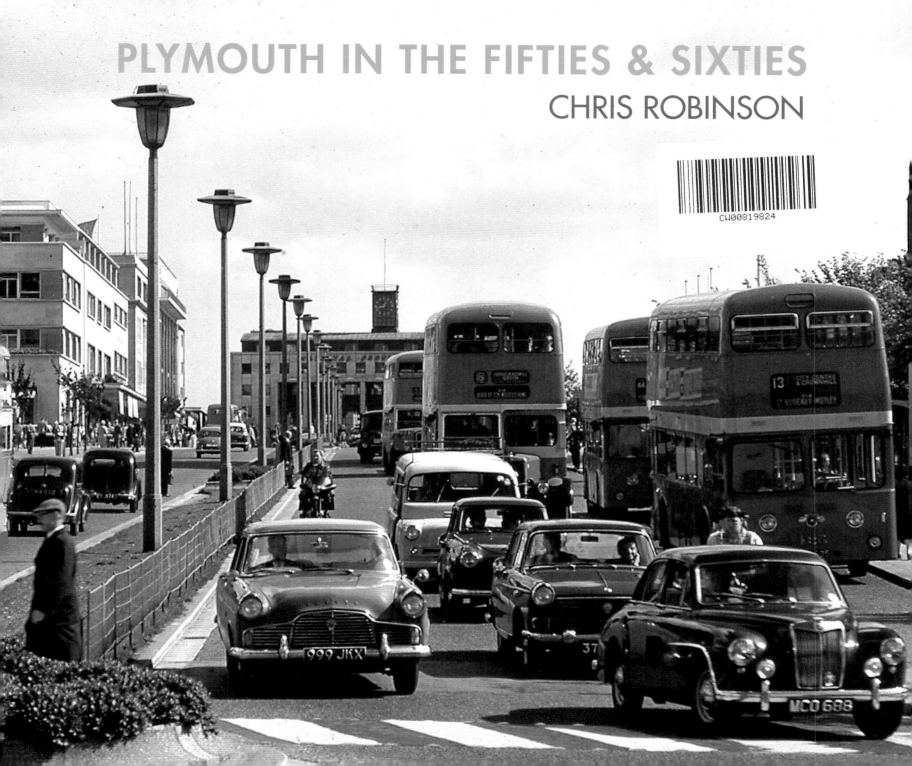

PLYMOUTH IN THE FIFTIES & SIXTIES

CHRIS ROBINSON

British Library Cataloguing in Publication Data

Chris Robinson
Plymouth in the Fifties and Sixties

A catalogue record for this book is available from the British Library

ISBN 978-0-9569858-1-1

Written and illustrated by Chris Robinson
Layout Chris Robinson
Cover design Ben Robinson
© Chris Robinson 2012

First published 2012

Published by
Pen & Ink Publishing
34 New Street, Barbican
Plymouth PL1 2NA
Tel: 01752 705337/228120
Fax: 01752 770001
www.chrisrobinson.co.uk

Printed and bound in Great Britain by
Latimer Trend & Company Ltd
Estover Close
Plymouth PL6 7PL
Devon

CONTENTS

INTRODUCTION

Plymouth in the Fifties and Sixties picks up where the previous volume - Plymouth in the Forties and Fifties - left off, that is, sometime around 1956-57. By that stage much of the rebuilding of the central area of the City Centre had been completed, but there was still plenty of work ongoing around the perimeter. There was also the important matter of reconstructing St Andrew's Church and the Guildhall.

This book looks at all those areas; around Western Approach, Cobourg Street, Charles Street, Exeter Street and Royal Parade.

It was in the late-Fifties that the impressive architectural punctuation mark, the National Provincial Bank, appeared at the eastern end of Royal Parade, and that the Drake Cinema, the Pannier Market and the Co-operative House, were built or completed at the other end. Meanwhile the early Sixties saw the erection of the City's first really tall buildings; the Civic Centre, the new office accommodation at North Road Station and the three tower blocks at Devonport.

The early Sixties also saw the City bid a fond farewell to a number of much-loved blitz survivors, among them the original Drake Circus with the Guinness Clock, the Harvest Home pub and the Odeon (formerly the Regent) cinema - where Bill Haley came to play for his doting fans in February 1957.

Royal Parade, 1958.

The Fifties and Sixties, were, after all, the birthplace of the baby boom, rock'n'roll generation and Plymouth had its fair share of skiffle bands and beat groups, coffee bars and clubs. Some were frequented by young lads with scooters, some, young lads with motor bikes, some, just young lads ... and lasses.

The Swinging Sixties marked a clear coming of age of the teenager, a relatively new arrival in society. These young people, with a little bit of time on their hands and money in their pockets, were soon the target of marketeers and they were swiftly parted with their money in an increasingly varied number of ways - with music, clothing, cosmetics and hair arrangements to the fore.

The youthful attitude to change and fashion was by no means confined to teenagers though; Plymouth Argyle with its youngest chairman to date - the Cash and Carry man, Robert Daniel - and its youngest manager - Malcolm Allison - went through a major re-branding exercise, adopting the Mayflower ship motif for the club's badge and a Euro-style hoop on their shirts. Not that the new kit had a hugely beneficial effect on their performances, nevertheless Home Park was the scene of many exciting moments through the period, notably when Jimmy Greaves made his first appearance back on British soil

in a reserve match for Tottenham Hotspur in December 1961.

Nearly 13,000 turned out to watch Bill Nicholson's £99,999 signing along with most of the nation's sporting press. At that point it had been one of the biggest crowds of the season at the ground, however, just a few weeks later, in January 1962, some 40,000 fans squeezed into the ground to watch Spurs' first team, in the 4th round of the FA Cup. Spurs were the current cup holders, indeed in the previous season they had become the first team in the twentieth century to do the league and cup double. There was then no bigger team in the country - and predictably the visitors won, comfortably, with Greaves scoring twice in their 5-1 victory.

Greaves was in action again at Home Park a few seasons later, again playing to a full house, this time as part of the English League team who put 12 goals past an Irish League team. Probably even more exciting than seeing the goals go in, however, was the opportunity to see England's three West Ham World Cup stars, Bobby Moore, Geoff Hurst and Martin Peters, parading the Jules Rimet trophy around the ground.

Central Park was a scene of a great deal of activity throughout the Sixties as Plymouth Zoo was opened just behind the Barn Park end of Argyle's ground, and the City's first indoor pool was built near the Milehouse entrance to the park. The pools at Mount Wise and at Tinside were still hugely popular though and regularly attracted great crowds. The biggest crowd of the decade however swarmed the Hoe on 28 May 1967 to witness the return of the lone yachtsman Sir Francis Chichester as he completed the first single-stop circumnavigation of the world. It was a memorable occasion and well over 100,000 people were estimated to have watched from one vantage point or another around the Sound, and I was one of them.

Plymouth's population around that time was a little under 250,000 and included the newly embraced Plympton and Plymstock, both of which had, somewhat reluctantly, became a part of the expanding city on 1 April 1967.

Where once there had been a number of towns and villages in this area, now they were all subsumed under the Plymouth banner, and, as if to add insult to injury, the Sixties also saw Plympton and Plymstock, and Devonport, Keyham, Oreston and Turnchapel, all lose their railway stations as Dr Beeching's axe made major cuts in the provision of local and national railway services.

Royal Parade. St Andrew's has been restored and work on the Guildhall is almost finished.

People were so proud of their new City Centre that they were more than happy to just sit in the sun and admire it!

Of course, back then there was only one provider for such services - British Rail, just as there was only one electricity provider locally - the South Western Electricity Board. And one gas provider - South Western Gas Board. There was only one phone operator too, the GPO - General Post Office - who were also solely responsible for all our post.

Life was so much simpler then, and for those who had telephones you were unlikely to be bothered by someone trying to sell you cheaper electricity, gas, phone calls or line rental. Banking and insurance was more straightforward too as people seemed to spend more time living and less time agonising about how they should be living.

There was not a lot of choice in the world of radio and television either. The BBC expanded their wireless transmissions in 1967 when out of the old Light Programme, Home Service, and Third Programme, they fashioned Radios 1, 2, 3 and 4. This was mainly to counteract the influence of pop pirate stations, like Radio London and Radio Caroline. A month or two earlier in 1967 also saw the nation's third of only three TV Channels, BBC 2, become the first station in Europe to broadcast regularly in colour. Not that it affected too many people at first, especially if they were tied in to a black and white rental agreement.

Locally it was of more interest that the BBC and our local ITV franchise holders, Westward, had, at the beginning of the Sixties, both launched their own magazine style evening news programmes - Spotlight and Westward Diary.

Among the first stories they would have covered were the last journey of the Saltash Ferry and the first crossing of the Tamar Road Bridge at the end of October 1961. The flags were out on both sides of the Tamar as the new crossing spelt an end to the hours of queuing that motorists had had to deal with at various times of the year - and the lack of any sort of service in the small hours of the morning.

The local road infrastructure received plenty of attention throughout the Fifties and Sixties, particularly in the wake of the closure of so many rail routes. There was an improvement to the access into the South Hams via the new bridge over the Laira, which was also opened in 1961. There were improvements to the northern route in and out of the City with the construction of the Crownhill by-pass towards the end of the Sixties and numerous other modifications here and there as the A38 was upgraded to rival the previous main artery deep into

These were heady times: our modern shopping centre was more or less completed and our old quarter, the area we now know generally as the Barbican, was saved from almost total destruction by the timely intervention of a group of men who came to call themselves the Plymouth Barbican Association (now Trust).

Curiously enough it is thanks almost entirely to that trust that we can bring you many of the images that you see in this tome, for it was in 2007 to celebrate their 50th anniversary, that the Directors of the Trust decided to found and fund the South West Image Bank. Without it thousands, millions even, of negatives and photographic images might have been lost forever, including many of those that appear here. Alas we do not know the names of some of the photographers who took the many wonderful colour images, but we hope you will agree that it is an absolute delight to see an era that for the most part was recorded in black and white, brought back to life in glorious colour.

The cars, the clothes, the places and the people are all ready reminders of what to many will seem like only yesterday, and yet to others will be at least a lifetime away. Whichever group you belong to I hope you enjoy reading this as much as I have putting it all together!

Chris Robinson *October 2012*

This is the modern world - Royal Parade and shiny red double deckers.

Royal Parade c1960 - both the Guildhall and St Andrew's have been restored and work has begun on the site for the Civic Centre.

THE CITY CENTRE

By the time work actually began on the construction of the City's new Council offices in 1959 the rest of the City Centre had more or less been laid out according to the proposals in the Plan for Plymouth that the City Engineer, James Paton-Watson, and the celebrated town planner, Patrick Abercrombie, had produced in 1943 and that the Council had approved in 1944.

However 18 years had now passed since the Luftwaffe had largely flattened the heart of the City and ideas about the future were starting to change. The proposals expressed in 1943 had been to create a civic precinct between Royal Parade and Notte Street, populated with buildings that echoed the proportions of those new structures on the northern side of Royal Parade, but on a grander scale.

The main civic buildings were to be *'grouped around an enlarged Westwell Street Gardens,'* most of which are preserved. Thus the splendid trees which had survived the Blitz would be preserved for all time.

'The main civic group would comprise Municipal Buildings and a Council Chamber on the west side with Law Courts and Guildhall on the east.

'The condition of the remains of the pre-war Municipal Buildings and Guildhall precludes their being rebuilt, although the Tower might be preserved and embodied in the future buildings.'

1959: The view from Princess Square looking down towards those trees in Westwell Gardens and the surviving properties in Westwell Street, including the doomed Humm's showroom, built in the late 1930s.

Top: *Demolition work in Westwell Street. Middle and bottom: Work begins on the Civic Centre site.*

However that was not the view of Hector Stirling who, in 1950, was appointed City Architect.

That same summer, the Minister of Works, Richard Stokes, visited the City and recommended that *'the whole building be knocked down and a fresh start made.'* But no such move was made and the following year the Reconstruction Committee, led by Sir Clifford Tozer, took the decision to rebuild the Guildhall, and Stirling, who was then in his early 40s, was charged with the task.

The execution was done without the same deference that had been visited upon St Andrew's Church and although the basic structure was maintained Stirling relocated the entrance of the building to face what was destined to become the modern equivalent of the old Guildhall Square.

The new entrance with its *'undulating, coffered canopy'* was *'distinctly modern'*, but *'the drama was reserved for lobbies and the great hall where he created one of the best and richest interiors of the 1950s'* (Jeremy Gould, Plymouth: Vision of a Modern City).

Just as that reconstruction was being planned, so, in one of the world's most modern cities of all, New York, Gordon Bunshaft and Natalie de Blois were overseeing the construction of their *'quintessential and seminal glass-box skyscraper'*, Lever House.

Completed in 1952, as the American HQ of Lever Brothers, the British soap giants, this building was to inspire several European structures, including the South Terminal of the Paris-Orly airport, in 1961, the Europa Center in Berlin, in 1965, and, sometime between the two, Plymouth's own Civic Centre.

Stirling first came up with designs for the building in 1954. His proposals showed a 14-storey tower with a glass-curtain wall facade - just like the Lever building. His plan, in his own words, was for a scheme *'grouping a large number of public buildings in such a manner to give a feeling of spaciousness and vitality at a focal point in the City Centre, and to present to the moving eye of the viewer a continuously interesting series of visual compositions both in height and depth.'*

In the event Stirling revised his designs three times, always making sure that he was staying true to the spirit of the 1943 Plan.

'His proposed buildings were required by the plan to balance in scale with the Guildhall and the tower of St Andrew's Church; Royal Parade had been influenced by Princess Street in Edinburgh and the

1959: work is underway on the construction of the Civic Centre, the Guildhall is restored, but there are still one or two pre-war properties - and post-war pre-fabs - standing in Westwell Street.

Top: HJW Stirling's 1954 proposals for Plymouth's new Civic Centre. Bottom: The building takes shape.

Municipal Buildings had to follow the idea that the shops and offices north of the carriageway should be balanced by the monuments - the civic buildings and the church - south of the carriageway. The 'towers' of each monument were designed to visually link with each other so that when viewed from the North (i.e. from the proposed railway station) and from Lorimar's Naval War Memorial to the South, they would stand side by side and at an appropriate scale in height and length apart. The Civic Centre also had to be seen from any point in the City Centre so that it was an immediately identifiable landmark and one that could be used as a point of navigation' (Graham Hobbins - The Civic Centre).

This all sounded great on paper, but increasingly the Council were becoming frustrated by the fact that the plans weren't really progressing. Stirling complained that not only had he not been asked for any detailed designs, but that his department was understaffed and underpaid and busy dealing with the pressing demands from the local authority for housing.

And so it was that in 1957 the well-known landscape architect, Geoffrey Jellicoe, of Jellicoe, Ballantyne & Coleridge, was brought in to complete the designs. Jellicoe, who had become the founding President of the International Federation of Landscape Architects in 1948, was well aware of Stirling's plans, having been a member of the Royal Fine Art Commission that had approved the designs in the first place.

Jellicoe was happy to help realise the project, but was also keen to ensure that it was executed in accordance with Stirling's original proposals *'in spirit as well as in reality.'*

However the floating glass facade was replaced with two-tone concrete panels cast in local granite aggregate, the base became faced in riven Delabole slate, and inside the walls were faced in dark Ashburton marble, all helping to give the end product a more indiginous feel.

Perhaps Jellicoe and Ballantyne's most significant departure from the original design however was the striking butterfly roof that sheltered the popular top-floor public restaurant - a facility that afforded all Plymothians the opportunity to view their bright new city from a stunning vantage point.

The other major change, of course, was the axing of the proposed Treasury Department that was to have run along the western stretch of Royal Parade - a victim of the late-Fifties 'credit squeeze'.

Work in progress - note the bus stops on the far right.

The scaffolding starts to come down and the Civic Centre is about to become a front cover-icon.

The Civic Centre and Council House, imaginatively linked by Jellicoe's deftly designed spaces incorporating the ancient trees of Westwell Gardens, made a massive impact on the public psyche. This was truly the crowning glory to Plymouth's post-war redevelopment and a fitting memorial to the people of Plymouth who lived through the war: *'The little man and his wife'* as Pat Twyford put it in his book about the war years, *'John Citizen, who discarded his bowler hat for steel helmet, his umbrella for the stirrup-pump, who set aside his mild manner and rolled up his sleeves when the supreme job had to be done …'*

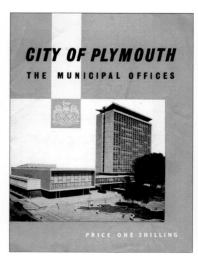

Geoffrey Jellicoe's landscaped square, incorporating the old trees of Westwell Gardens, complements the new Civic Centre.

Plymouth's first skyscraper is complete and the flags are out.

The Plymouth that arose from the ashes was the envy of many local authorities and the achievement was recognised at the highest level when in March 1960 the Duke of Edinburgh came down to unveil the tablet in the Council House that serves as a foundation stone; an action that was capped two years later, in July 1962, when the Queen officially declared the Council House open.

Clockwise from top left: *Civic Centre from Derry's Cross; Queen Elizabeth II and the Duke of Edinburgh arrive to open the new Council House and Civic Centre; Opening day; the foyer of the new Civic Centre..*

The evening sun lights up the great green swathe that now leads up to the top of the Hoe.

The uncluttered open spaces that were now available for everyone to enjoy were in marked contrast to the narrow streets and restricted vistas that had characterised pre-war Plymouth. Indeed few cities in England were as open and inviting as Plymouth now appeared. With the Hoe, a public open space of unparalleled natural beauty, at the end of the great new boulevard that was Armada Way, Plymouth's offer, with its state-of-the-art shopping centre, was huge. Visitors came from all over the westcountry to shop, and tourists from all over the country came to admire.

The detailing in and around the new civic complex was particularly rich and rewarding, and although the main materials used in the cladding of the Civic Centre were obtained locally, much of the internal fabric was comparatively exotic with a whole range of African and other hardwood veneers pressed into service, from the Agba to Zebrano, including Avodire, Courbaril, Muhuhu and Opepe.

Other interesting features included Italian mosaics with glass from Murano, a Thermal Storage Plant (using cheap off-peak electricity to heat the building - rare in the Sixties) and the first PABX4 telephone system, with satellite exchanges, to be installed in England.

And, of course, these were only the council offices, the Council House itself was another wonder in its own right.

Left: *The spiral staircase at the back of the Civic Centre.* Middle: *One of the ornamental ponds.* Right: *The front entrance and first-floor gallery space.*

Top: *The top of the main staircase in the Council House.* Bottom: *The Council Chamber.*

The spaces and proportions of the Council House are redolent of the Festival of Britain fever that gripped the country at the dawn of the 1950s, as is the artwork that decorates different areas of the building.

The entrance and lobby, like its neighbour, was finished in a variety of unusual hardwoods, while a series of glazed screens showcase marine-themed engravings by the New Zealand-born artist John Hutton who achieved great fame for his glass engravings (ten years in the making) on the Great West Screen of Coventry Cathedral - work that was also completed in 1962.

At the top of the impressive cantilevered staircase is a giant plaster relief of the Plymouth Coat of Arms by David Weeks (examples of whose work can also be seen in the Guildhall and Pannier Market). The Council Chamber itself is decorated with the work of German-born artist Hans Tisdall - Tisdall had settled in Britain when he was just out of his teens in 1930.

Commissioned by Jellicoe himself, Tisdall's pieces depict various aspects of Plymouth's history, from the civic - the mace, baton, and coat of arms; through the maritime - Drake's standard, flag and arms; to the arms of Devonport, the Eddystone lighthouse and the Plymouth seal. A popular children's book illustrator and artist, Tisdall, interestingly enough, also designed the dust jacket for Garrett Mattingly's celebrated book about *The Defeat of the Spanish Armada* (first published in 1959).

Tisdall also designed the original wall curtains in the Reception Room. Meanwhile, another striking and significant piece of original artwork is the Mary Adshead mosaic in the Member's entrance hall. Adshead had already designed a major piece for Plymstock Church - St Mary's - in 1957. The Council House mosaic, however, was full of historic rather than religious imagery and again included many references to Plymouth's maritime past - King Billy, Drake's circumnavigation, the Mayflower, the Brunel Bridge, the Eddystone …

Perhaps the most famous artist of all to be involved in the post-war reconstruction of the City, though, was John Egerton Christmas Piper.

Piper had been an official war artist and produced his first painting of bomb damage the morning after an air-raid destroyed Coventry Cathedral. Later, and together with Patrick Reyntiens, John Piper designed the stained-glass windows for the new Coventry Cathedral. Meanwhile, here in Plymouth, where the decision was taken to restore the mother church rather than leave it as a war memorial (as they did with the original Coventry Cathedral and with Charles Church in Plymouth), Piper worked with Reyntiens (who worked up the designs in glass) on the east windows of the restored St Andrew's Church.

The strikingly modern and rather abstract designs were in marked contrast to the traditional approach that the English architect Frederick Etchells had taken towards the rest of the restoration. Having said that, the west window, dedicated to the memory of Lord Astor (who died in 1952 and who had been a driving force in planning and realising the plans for post-war Plymouth) is somewhat more figurative.

That window was erected soon after the re-consecration and re-opening of the church, which was on St Andrew's Day, Friday 30 November, 1957.

Left: *St Andrew's organist of many years, Harry Moreton.* Top: *The restored Mother Church and Guildhall.*
Bottom: *Inside the restored St Andrew's.*

23

While there had been comparatively few questions raised about the restoration of St Andrew's, the debate over whether the Guildhall should be brought back into use, or demolished, raged for many years before the Council ultimately ruled in favour of its being kept. The fate of the Municipal Building also, albeit briefly, hung in the balance, but as the line of Royal Parade would have been compromised by its retention, it went.

So it was that a fully restored Guildhall was opened on 24 September 1959, by Field Marshall Montgomery, British commander at El Alamein and chief planner of the D Day invasion of Normandy.

Queen Elizabeth the Queen Mother also visited the newly restored building. Escorted by the Lord Mayor, she was able to admire another new series of post-war windows, this time painted by the New Zealand-born war artist FH Coventry. The 14 designs depict different scenes from the City's history, while the three great chandeliers that grace the main hall represent each of the Three Towns of Plymouth, Stonehouse and Devonport.

The marvellous Gobelin tapestry that graces the far wall, is based on a Raphael cartoon, and was originally a gift from Napoleon III to Lord Clarendon: it is on permanent loan to the city.

Top left: *The Queen Mother inspects the new Guildhall with Lord Mayor Percy Washbourn and Alderman Arthur Goldberg,* Above: *Lord Mayor and Queen Mother outside.* Bottom left: *A view of the Council House looking across Princess Street.*

Of course Plymouth City Council hadn't been the only organisation to get bombed out of their pre-war base, it happened to a great many, including the YMCA (Young Man's Christian Association): the Plymouth branch was damaged beyond repair, while the Devonport YMCA was compulsorily purchased by the Admiralty. After sharing premises for a few years in the former Hoe Mansions Hotel, permission was granted to allow the construction of an all new, 102-bedroom YMCA facility at the top of Armada Way.

Above: *1958: the Duke of Edinburgh arrives in Plymouth to officially open the new YMCA building at the junction of Armada Way and Cobourg Street.* Top right: *The Duke with the Lord Mayor, George Wingett, on Royal Parade, 29 July 1958.* Bottom right: *The Armada Way elevation.*

The new Law Courts complete with a Flemish glass and concrete screen above the main entrance, that 'admits light to the main hall and provides a coloured mosaic background for the Civic Arms wrought in gilt metal.'.

Still in Armada Way, another collaboration between Hector Stirling and Jellicoe, Ballantyne & Coleridge, was the Crown Court and Police Station complex that was built by Costain Construction across from the Council House and opened the year the Civic Centre was completed.

Lord Denning PC, the then Right Honourable Master of the Rolls, officiated at the ceremony which took place on Tuesday 16 April 1963. The development virtually completed the provision of the civic facilities that had been lost during the war and concentrated them in an area south of Royal Parade, leaving all the shops and commercial offices on the northern side of the line.

The northern end of Armada Way was still incomplete, but the other great axis of the new City Centre - Royal Parade - was now virtually finished - only the site that had been earmarked for the Treasury block remained undeveloped.

At the eastern end a flurry of activity in the late-Fifties had seen Cyril Pinfold's designs for the main Post Office realised in 1957 and, the following year, in September, the punctuation mark for Plymouth's *'most stately avenue'*, the National Provincial Bank, was opened to the public.

Top: Under construction, Plymouth's new Post Office. Bottom: c1960 - The Post Office is finished, as is the new stretch of Exeter Street across Bretonside.

Three years in the construction, the bank was designed by BC Sherren (with assistance from staff architects Norman, Souter and Miles). Sherren was then the principal staff architect with the National Provincial and the building was designed, not just as a branch bank but as the regional HQ of the National Provincial – hence the grand scale and the comparatively substantial budget available for the project.

Faced, like the rest of the new buildings on the north side of Royal Parade, in Portland stone, the front elevation was more classically inspired than most and its main feature was the impressive stripped portico of Devon granite. Behind this, the exterior wall of the entrance was decorated with delightful coloured mosaics, littered with small golden images of anchors, fish, castles and squirrels, acknowledging the bank's coat of arms.

Above it all a curved copper roof sat surmounted by a translucent green glass lantern clock that lined up perfectly with the avenue it looked out over.

If the roof of the Civic Centre building afforded viewers the perfect vantage point to look up and down Armada Way, then the National Provincial Bank balcony provided the same service for anyone anxious to take stock of the other great axis of the new centre of the city, Royal Parade.

With a sizeable roundabout at either end of the tree-lined boulevard it's interesting to speculate on the degree to which Sherren may have modelled his clock feature on the mini-tower that capped the slightly earlier headquarters of the South Western Gas Board which also lines up perfectly with the central reservation of Royal Parade.

Whether it was all part of some master plan or not - like the towers of Dingles and the Pearl Assurance at the meeting point of Royal Parade and Armada Way - there could be no denying that this was about as impressive as any town or city centre could get and it became a popular and much photographed picture postcard view of modern Britain. Plymothians could be justly proud of their phoenix rising from the ashes. The old towers on the south of the line did balance with the bold new neighbouring Civic Centre - it all worked.

Top: A magnificent punctuation mark appears at the eastern end of Royal Parade - the National Provincial Bank.
Bottom: Plymouth's new Post Office on the edge of St Andrew's Cross Roundabout.

Early 1962. Royal Parade is almost complete and the scaffolding around the Civic Centre is slowly coming down.

A picture that appears to have been taken from the scaffolding around Charles Church tower showing work on the bus station progressing along with the construction of the viaduct that would run across the top of the shops and offices below.

Beyond the bank and the Post Office the situation was a little less obvious. The clearance of the buildings at the top of Treville Street, in late 1957, had opened up the vista between St Andrew's Cross roundabout and Charles Church. The plan here was to create a wide viaduct underneath and beyond which a new bus station would be created for the City.

By the beginning of March 1958 the new stretch was open. It was styled Exeter Street, as it now represented the new route towards that city, and superseded what had been the old western end of Exeter Street.

For over 20 years the completion of one building project would be immediately followed by work on another project - there was always a building site somewhere in the City Centre.

Top and bottom: Bretonside bus station, clean, bright and new.

Later that month, on Sunday 30 March, Bretonside Bus Station came into operation for the first time. The first bus out of Bretonside that morning was Western National service 88 which left the bus station a little after 5am with just one passenger on board - Eric Watson - a Hoe resident who was on his way to Ivybridge, to work at Moorhaven Hospital.

It's interesting to note that around this time the Joint Services Committee agreed to renumber the services numbered in the 80s and 90s and bring them within the 1 to 57 range - a move that also allowed them to eliminate a number of 'a' and 'b' suffixes from the city's bus services.

There were other changes too, not only with regard to renumbering, but also in regard to routes - an inevitable by-product of the post-war redevelopment of the City, the inevitable population shifts and the new estates.

For the most part the buses from Bretonside were headed out of town, to Plympton, Plymstock, the South Hams and the new estates: Ernesettle, Honicknowle, Southway, Tamerton and Whitleigh.

Initially Western National, Embankment Motors, the Plymouth Co-operative Society and Heybrook Bay Motors each had a shop on the main concourse and operated excursions from here.

That situation didn't last long, however: in December 1959 Heybrook Bay Motor Services sold out to Western National and the two routes they had run - to Heybrook Bay and Bovisand - became Plymouth joint services 54 and 55.

Meanwhile Western National lost no time in selling on the Heybrook Bay fleet, a move Embankment Motors emulated two years later, in December 1961, when that company bought out the Co-operative Society Motors operation. Initially they disposed of all but seven of the Co-op's fleet, the seven all being Leylands, which were hastily repainted in the brown and beige Embankment livery.

However, after just one season, these too were disposed of, as it was policy on the part of Embankment to only use Bedford vehicles.

Prior to the construction of Bretonside there had been a temporary bus station on the town side of the railway embankment leading to Millbay, and here too there was a great amount of development in the late-Fifties, early-Sixties.

Bretonside in the sun.

After the Blitz the area around the comparatively newly built ABC Royal (1938) was left relatively untouched for the best part of 20 years. Nissen huts were erected on the site of the bomb damaged Theatre Royal Hotel and these served for a number of years as the Plymouth NAAFI club. The gutted Athenaeum on the other side was gradually removed and various other bomb sites were cleared. But apart from that a number of other wartime survivors, notably in Athenaeum Lane and the western end of George Street (Genoni's foremost among them), enjoyed a last hurrah before the demolition men moved in.

Furthermore, just to the west of the old Athenaeum building, the pleasant park that lined the front of the Crescent was also bounded by the line of George Street, stopping just short of the Continental Hotel on the corner of Buckland Street, it's mature trees providing one of the few green lungs in the heart of the City.

But not for much longer, as the 1943 Plan had identified part of this area as the Theatre Precinct of the new City Centre and an illustration in the Plan showed what was still then known as the Royal Cinema with two other cultural and entertainment buildings, of similar style and proportion, alongside it. The Plan also showed a major road behind this area, although little did the planners appear to anticipate quite what a busy thoroughfare it would soon become, as Notte Street was extended into a new road - the Crescent - which cut right through the early nineteenth-century park. Before long all these fine trees would be gone.

Athenaeum Place runs around the back of the ABC cinema. The line of pre-war George Street is still clearly discernible at the front of the building as is the park in front of the Crescent on the other side.

Work began on clearing the remaining properties at the eastern end of Union Street, beyond the temporary bus station, in 1956. The flagship building on this site was to be 20th Century Fox's first British cinema - it was also the first, and as it transpired, the only post-war cinema to be built in the City. Indeed it may well have been the first post-war single-screen cinema in the country. It had been the intention of 20th Century Fox to make it the first of the American film company's chain of cinemas across Europe, but in the event it was the only one to be realised.

The architect was Leonard Allen, who had already worked on a number of cinemas, in Sidcup, London, and in 1948, in Egypt where he designed the Tivoli Cinema for Rank in Cairo.

Above: *The site is cleared for the new Drake Cinema.*
Right: *View from the top of Co-operative House.*

The 1600-seater Drake Cinema was opened on 6 June 1958 by the Lord Mayor George Wingett. The programme on that day saw a screening of the Plymouth Story - a tribute to the people of Plymouth and the building of the city of tomorrow - alongside a special charity showing of 20th Century Fox's latest blockbuster - South Pacific.

The first full programme starred Pat Boone and Shirley Jones in April Love, with the Plymouth Story again on the bill.

The following month South Pacific returned for it's scheduled run and remarkably took up residence in the projection room for the next six months - a local record.

The story goes, incidentally, that 20th Century Fox only built the Drake because they had made so much money with two shows in London, at the Rialto and the Carlton, but weren't able to take the money out of the country.

The venture didn't seem to work for the company however, and sometime early in 1960 Fox sold the cinema to the Rank Organisation.

By that time most of the perimeter of the new Derry's Cross Roundabout had been developed.

View from the Civic Centre looking down Union Street towards Devonport. The railway lines into Millbay run across the scene like a dark scar. In the foreground a garage and car park are under construction.

Occupying a prime site on the corner of Raleigh Street was the Plymouth and South Devon Savings Bank. The bank headquarters had previously been housed in the well-loved Prudential Building that had survived the Blitz despite severe bomb damage. For safety's sake the bank had made duplicate copies of all their records in 1939, but happily these were never needed. However although the red brick Prudential building had remained in business throughout the war, it had become increasingly isolated and, in 1951, it was pulled down to make way for the Pearl Assurance building.

Temporary accommodation for the bank was found in a couple of Nissen huts in York Street where the long mahogony counter, salvaged from the Prudential building, was installed.

The following year the Derry's Cross site was secured for the new HQ but steel shortages prevented any work being started and it wasn't until 24 April 1956 that the new bank was completed and opened by Lord Mackintosh of Halifax.

Harold Mackintosh was then the national leader of the savings movement and coincidentally that year had overseen the introduction of the Premium Bond. He had also inherited the Mackintosh confectionery business (the Quality Street people) on the death of his father in 1920.

The new premises, incidentally, housed a modified version of the old mahogany counter - it had been given a slight curve to match the new building.

Three years after the opening, on 21 May 1959, the bank became the HQ of the newly merged Plymouth and Devonport banks, henceforth known as the Plymouth, Devonport and Cornwall Trustee Savings Bank. Curiously enough, the Devonport Bank had been the bigger of the two, but by now it was clear that there wasn't going to be a new shopping centre built in Devonport and that Stoke, where the Devonport board had set up its head office, was never going to be anything more than a suburban centre.

Here at the opening to Raleigh Street, meanwhile, they were directly opposite the largest of the post-war department stores, Co-operative House, the headquarters of the Plymouth Co-operative Society, which, in January 1960, celebrated its centenary in the City with the opening of its new restaurant and cafeteria - the Dolphin - on the third floor, overlooking Royal Parade.

Top: *Derry's Cross with Austin House and the Plymouth and South Devon Savings Ban* Bottom: *A wider view from the top of the Civic Centre looking down on the old and no isolated Civil Defence Headquarters, which had been at the Union Street end of Bank England Place.* Right: *Co-operative House c1968 with the Dolphin Restaurant inset.*

The Pannier Market nears completion while Raleigh Street still has some way to go, although the Plymouth and South Devon Savings Bank is ready for business.

Another major player to realise that Devonport's future was not destined to be as rosy post-war as it had been before was Sir Clifford Tozer.

Tozers had been one of the big shopping names in pre-war Devonport, along with Boold's and Love's, and for many years a hope was cherished that Devonport might be blessed with a new post-war shopping centre. Indeed as late as 1953, when Clifford Tozer was serving the City as Lord Mayor, a meeting of Devonport Traders agreed to recommend to Plymouth City Council's Reconstruction Committee that *'the shopping areas of Devonport should be largely situated within the Fore-street, Marlborough-street, Albert-road, Tavistock-road, Stoke, districts.'*

Sir Clifford Tozer favoured Marlborough Street, handy for people from Torpoint and those who were rehoused in Pembroke Street and the Granby Barracks site.

However it wasn't to be and in the end Tozer's post-war presence became a brand new store facing out across the line of Raleigh Street, right next door to Plymouth's Pannier Market.

Significant among the new buildings in the City Centre as being the only major development to be designed by a local firm, the Pannier Market was built to the plans of Messrs Walls & Pearn of Halwell Street (CHP Pearn and HF Walls would also come to design the Athenaeum Theatre and Lecture Hall).

The Market is significant as it probably has the most architecturally interesting interior in the City Centre.

With help from their inspired structural engineer Albin Chronowicz, they created a vast open space that was over 12 metres high, thanks to seven substantial concrete spans that stretch out across a distance of nearly 46 metres. It was a remarkable achievement and the Pannier Market has come to occupy a position of some renown in architectural circles on account of it, and Chronowicz published a book the year that the Market opened, 1959, entitled *'The Design of Shells'*.

The Market is now trading, as is Tozers - one of the few stores to make the move across from Devonport.

Another striking feature of the new market building was the artwork of David Weeks in the entrance porches. The first sight the general public had of these new wonders was on Monday 7 September 1959. With its gentle curves the new building was unlike anything else north of Royal Parade, although like the refashioned Guildhall entrance, it did have something of that Festival of Britain feel to it, a feeling that was further enhanced by Weeks' very contemporary, and simply coloured, allegorical murals.

These are not simply paintings, but are works of art set into the plaster of the wall and then filled with paint.

The use of simple primary colours for the murals was originally echoed in the canary yellow canopy, the blue ceiling, and in the tiling of the exterior elevations, not just of the Pannier Market, but also of the facades of the shops and flats around the Market and in Frankfort Gate. This was, of course, one of the few areas of the post-war City where there was a mix of retail and residential.

Top: *Plymouth's striking new Pannier Market.* Bottom left: *Opening day, 1959.* Right: *David Weeks' entrance mural.* Opposite page: *The Market from Cornwall Street.*

Frankfort Gate, both in name and layout, appeared to be offering itself up as the western entry point into the new City Centre, but for all that there was no vehicular access and, initially, no obvious pedestrian route into the area across the busy dual-carriageway of Western Approach..

The original Frankfort Gate had been pulled down in 1783 and the street and avenues adjoining had been considerably widened and improved.

Frankfort Street, Frankfort Lane and Frankfort Square were all well known to the pre-war generation of Plymothians, but not only was the gate long gone but its location was some way to the east of the space that now bore the name, up in Armada Way.

Frankfort Gate, so-called because at one time there was a fort by the original gate, commanded by a man called Frank, had however, always been the western entry point into the town and so the rationale for resurrecting the name for this new entry point was obvious enough.

In other respects, however, what had been the driving vision for the post-war City Centre - Portland stone, glass and a simple stylish look - was now being compromised by a brick and brightly coloured panel approach. The construction of the bottom end of the town was distinctly bottom end in every way. The mix of retail and residential was logical enough - Plymouth after all now had a relatively massive retail footprint and a rather generous helping of office space, particularly after the displaced pre-war shops and their administration departments were now vacating their temporary homes in North HIll, Mutley, Mannamead and beyond, but it meant that Frankfort Gate had more of a housing estate shopping area feel to it.

It wasn't a prime shopping area, but it was a haven for local, independent retailers and was largely free of the high street chains and multiples.

Left - top and bottom: *Frankfort Gate, designed by City Architect Hector Stirling and built by Laing - 1955-57.*

Looking across Market Avenue with an unusual and short-lived glimpse of Well Street. The space would soon be filled with one of only a handful of new pubs to be built in the City Centre. Meanwhile that section of Well Street would soon disappear forever.

The shift away from the materials that characterised the core area of Plymouth's new City Centre, was by no means unique to the western fringes - as the Sixties progressed there seemed to be a general free-for-all, with only the need to conform to a standard building height guiding the architects and planners. With scant regard for the sophisticated aesthetic considerations, the new shopping area was gradually surrounded by a mix of perfunctory properties that failed to frame the core in an attractive or imaginative way.

The stretch lining the eastern side of Western Approach was particularly disappointing and with hindsight it almost seems a slight rather than a compliment to have named the area behind it Colin Campbell Court, in supposed honour of the City's wartime and immediate post-war Town Clerk.

Colin Campbell had come to Plymouth from Burnley in 1935, the same year that James Paton Watson visited the City for the first time, and like Paton-Watson, Campbell had a major part to play in the redevelopment of the blitzed City.

However it had been Paton Watson who had been the driving force behind the decision to cut a clear wide path through the middle of the new City Centre. Paton Watson had been amazed to find out just how close the train station had been to the Hoe when he first arrived in Plymouth. The pre-war arrangement of streets gave little or no indication of the proximity to the seafront, and so when the opportunity arose he leapt at the chance to create an obvious link.

Above: *Western Approach defines the western boundary of the new City Centre.*
Right: *Armada Way with its three great 'collegiate' lawns.*

However although the planting was there to create a tree-lined boulevard right down the middle of what became Armada Way (other names mooted had included Phoenix Way and the People's Way) that bold vision has never quite been realised and instead pedestrians have ever been forced along the pavements. When it was first being laid out though, the potential for what could have been an even more striking feature was clear to see.

The idea of such a pedestrian-friendly thoroughfare was something of an anathema, though, in an era when more and more people were becoming car owners for the first time. The post-war baby boomers were not only hungry for the independence conferred by the motor car, they also wanted to be able to park their vehicles right next to where they wanted to be. New George Street, Cornwall Street and then Mayflower Street all crisscrossed Armada Way and there was even a vehicular loop just below Mayflower Street.

At first parking was on a casual basis, then the latest idea to be imported from America, where car ownership was ahead of the rest of the world, arrived - the parking meter.

Introduced into the UK in London in the summer of 1958, exactly 23 years after their debut in Oklahoma, the temperamental stick-mounted motoring monitors arrived in the City soon afterwards and by May 1964 drivers were deemed to have become sufficiently familiar with them for the local authorities to stop issuing warnings and to start making prosecutions.

Denis Percy Thompson was the first unhappy victim: he was fined £1 after pleading guilty to trying to put an extra sixpence in the slot after his allotted time was up.

As the modern world gradually insinuated itself across all aspects of the new shopping centre, so the last remnants of pre-war Plymouth were removed.

It was by no means an overnight affair, some buildings hung on more tenaciously than others. But gradually those surviving bits of Russell Street, Morley Street, and Cambridge Street disappeared and in 1962 the old Regent Cinema, known since 1940 as the Odeon, fell to the hands of the developer and Littlewoods appeared on its site.

Top: *Late pre-war survivors - but not for much longer - in Russell Street viewed from Armada Way.*
Bottom: *Armada Way, with plenty of open grass areas and newly planted trees.*

The junction of Armada Way and New George Street, with a happy mix of pedestrian and vehicular traffic.

Littlewoods started advertising for staff in the summer of 1964 - primarily they were looking for sales and cafe assistants, aged between 15 and 19, and a full-time assistant cook *'under age 40'.*

Although there was no hard and fast rule, New George Street, where Littlewoods had taken up residence, was dominated by department stores, clothing outlets and shoe shops, while a little to the north, the mainstays of Cornwall Street were grocers and butchers. This had been quite a deliberate decision on the part of the planners originally, but as time wore on the mix inevitably grew more varied. Jewellers were dotted around the centre and there was a large number of cafes similarly spread around, with Lyons and Goodbody's being among the most popular.

Stafford Williams' Magnet Restaurant in Cornwall Street (they had moved from Whimple Street having started out originally in Union Street) was another favourite haunt where many had their first proper dining-out experience, often as part of a works' Christmas outing.

Another popular local independent business was Yardley's music store towards the top end of Cornwall Street, opposite Halfords and John Temple.

Top: *Littlewoods built on the site of the former Regent Cinema (Odeon).* Bottom left: *Stafford Williams' Magnet Restaurant.* Right: *Yardley's music store, Cornwall Street.*
Opposite page: *Mayflower Street looking south-west.*

Above: *Mayflower Street nears completion. Note St Peter's and the Roman Catholic cathedral on the skyline.*
Left: *Jon Saberton's new menswear store in Mayflower Street opened in 1963.*

Meanwhile, although technically it was well within the designated area defining the new City Centre, Mayflower Street marking the main northern section of retail development, was, like Frankfort Gate and Western Approach, somewhat uninspiring and perfunctory.

One of the few havens of taste and style was Jon Saberton's menswear boutique, and even there most of the saving graces were on the inside.

It had been the retirement of Paton Watson in 1958 that had really freed up the developers from many of the post-war constraints that dictated a degree of uniformity for the City Centre. That, coupled with the end of rationing and of that period of post-war austerity that now ushered in a degree of affluence and a much wider range of materials generally.

Hence the introduction of colour that we'd already seen at Frankfort Gate.

'Strict regulation that was unquestioned in the early 1950s was less acceptable to a population of traders and developers who had "never had it so good" in the relatively affluent late 1950s. Perversely, less money was spent on buildings as private wealth increased. Developers realised that, as tenants not owner-occupiers, investment in expensive buildings and shop fitting was unnecessary' (Jeremy Gould - Plymouth Vision of a Modern City).

The appearance of the new buildings erected around the edges of the Portland stone-fronted heart of the City reflected this.

However one development that remained true to the original vision was the extension of Armada Way, right up to Cobourg Street and what would soon become North Cross roundabout and the creation of a Braille Garden.

Designed by Stirling again, in conjunction with the City Engineer's Department, the garden utilised stonework rescued from pre-war buildings and included a number of especially chosen aromatic plants that could be enjoyed by the blind and partially sighted, as well as the sighted.

Right top and bottom: *Armada Way - the wonderful new direct route from North Cross to the Hoe is almost finished.*

A casualty of the construction of the first multi-storey car park, built off Mayflower Street, to serve the new City Centre, was the late-Victorian South Western Hotel. Ironically this had been erected in 1877 in the wake of the opening of the then new railway station at North Road, and at the end of the 1960s, one of the main developments proposed in the plan and not yet realised, was a hotel to sit at the top of Armada Way. A hotel which hopefully would complement the expanded railway station that now occupied the North Road site.

The ground had been cleared, and was serving as an interim car park, but it would be another decade or so before work would begin.

Left: *The north-western stretch of Armada Way awaits completion and, in the meantime, serves as a car park.* Top: *Time was soon to be called on the South Western Hotel.* Bottom: *The southern side of Mayflower Street is completed.*

The top of York Street, with the Oporto pub on the left on the corner of William Street. Oxford Place is the turning off to the right in the middle distance.

The much-missed Oporto was another late victim of the post-war reconstruction: it was still standing in the early part of the summer of 1969, some 28 years after the Blitz had deprived it of so many of its neighbours.

One of half-a-dozen Pops or Popplestone & Co. public houses in the city at the time, it had celebrated more than a century on its site at the top of York Street.

York Street had been the main artery connecting the old City Centre with the New Town that had been created at the western end of Cobourg Street, in the first half of the nineteenth-century, and much of it had survived the war. Sadly, however, it all fell within the perimeter of the plan and once Western Approach had been cut through the old street pattern, taking out parts of Morley Place, Cambridge Street, King Gardens, Tracey Street and Well Street, its days were well and truly numbered.

The redevelopment had to stop somewhere though and several of the severed streets were left with their northern sections intact and somewhat isolated from the new City Centre, hence the construction of a major pedestrian underpass for people to negotiate this very busy ring road.

A wide line was being drawn around the new shopping area, and apart from the developments around Frankfort Gate and between there and the western end of Mayflower Street, there were very few people now living in that zone, where previously there had been thousands.

Top left: *The Oporto standing in not so splendid isolation.*
Right, top and bottom: *Early views of Western Approach.*

The Newtown Hotel and the Albion were among two dozen, or so, City Centre area pubs to be lost in the Fifties and Sixties.

It's hard now to imagine what Plymouth was like 200 years ago, but in 1814, there was very little development west of St Andrew's Church and north of Old Town Gate (where Marks and Spencer are today). The route to Devonport was via Millbridge or Stonehouse Lane (which later became King Street). Union Street did not exist and the area above Millbay was still shown as marshland. The tidal Stonehouse Creek stretched up to what is now Pennycomequick roundabout, where it met two streams running down from Tor and Houndiscombe, and North Road was a rural route known as Five Fields Lane. Also, at that time, the Cornishman, Richard Trevithick, was working on his steam locomotives, and George Stephenson had just produced his first steam engine design.

The industrial revolution was just about to step up another gear and Plymouth was going to witness the greatest period of expansion it had ever known. During the course of the nineteenth century the population would grow five or six fold, but in pure percentage terms the biggest change over that period was in the ten years between 1821 and 1831 when the number of Plymothians increased from a little over 21,000 to a little over 31,000 - that's almost 1,000 people per year and a 50% increase. All the more remarkable when you consider that in Drake's time, over 200 years earlier, the population was only around 7,000.

To put the figures in more concrete terms (or rather in terms of bricks and mortar) the number of houses in Plymouth in 1821 was 2,646 and ten years later that number had risen to 3,472 and the location of a goodly number of those 800 or so new houses was New Town.

The heart of New Town was at the junction of the road to Milehouse and the Saltash Ferry and the road running north of Barrack Street (soon known as York Street and Russell Street respectively).

The development, as you might expect from the name, wasn't confined to housing, however, there were plenty of shops and amenities and a number of pubs, among them the Albion and the New Town Hotel.

Top right: The doomed south-western section of Cobourg Street.
Bottom: Further east along Cobourg Street beyond the junction with York Street.

Inset: The development of the top end of Armada Way spells the end for a section of Cobourg Street...

The development was by no means confined to the area south of Cobourg Street either: the northern stretch was similarly lined with houses and, in the main street itself, commercial premises.

Belle Vue Corner stood, for many years after the war, at the western end of North Road East and here, shortly before demolition, you would have found Crook and Trott's wholesale newsagents and stationery, O'Brien's the opticians, Jack's photographic services, Belle Vue Television Service (the place for Eckovision) and Lavender Dry Cleaners.

A little further along Cobourg Street, towards Public Secondary, was Reed's motor showroom. Following the compulsory purchase by the local authority of his premises in 1969, Gilbert Reed, the managing director of the firm, voluntarily relinquished his main Ford dealership and thereby left Vospers Motor House to become the main dealer locally for Fords of Britain.

Reeds had been in Cobourg Street since 1924 and were just one of a number of victims of the widening of Cobourg Street and the creation of the major roundabout that was to become known as North Cross.

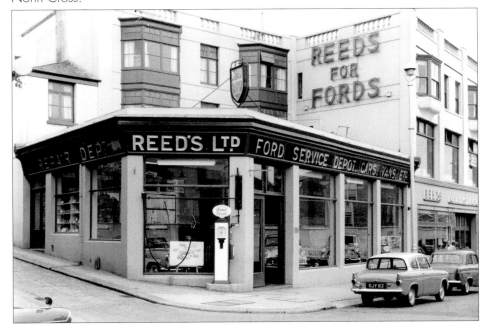

Left: *Belle Vue Corner at the junction of Cobourg Street and North Road East.*
Above: *Reed's Ford garage in Cobourg Street - note the Esso pump and the long -range hose.*

A little further along the road changes had already taken place with a mixture of mid-late Victorian premises being sacrificed for the last phases of the City Centre redevelopment.

One of the most lamented casualties of the process was the landmark hostelry on the corner of Tavistock Road and Pound Street (which ran into Cobourg Street) - the Harvest Home.

Built as a coaching house in the days when this stretch was still known as 'Old Town Without' the pub had a distinctive archway leading through to the stables. A sign recalling the bygone age of horse-drawn travel could be seen by the bell on the wall, to the side of the double doors leading through to the yard: it simply said 'Ring for Ostler' - the ostler being the man employed by Harvest Home to look after the horses.

A popular Plymouth hostelry, it was also where many students had their first pint, standing, as it did, just across the road from the old Tech College.

Planned in 1887 to commemorate Queen Victoria's Golden Jubilee, the Tech was opened in 1892 as the Victoria Jubilee Memorial Science, Art and Technical School, but quickly became the Plymouth Science, Art and Technical School. It wasn't long, however, before it had become more commonly known as Plymouth Tech, or simply 'the Tech.'

Standing on the site of the old cattle market (hence Pound Street) the building was designed by local architect, AD Shortridge and built by AR Debnam whose final bill came to a little over £6,000.

Plymouth wasn't overly blessed with academic institutions at the time and the new building was a very welcome, and state-of-the-art, affair fully equipped to take 'the lime-light lantern' which 'has come into vogue as an aid to education ... and a good deal of illustrations of lessons will be accomplished by its aid..'

Furthermore, in the classrooms 'at intervals on the wall, there are small patches of a substance known as black graphikos ... quite ready to receive the mark of chalk or pencil. By means of these a lecturer or teacher can move about among his pupils and impart lessons.'

Curiously enough 70-something years later when the old Tech was demolished, teachers still relied on much the same approach.

In 1914, in line with the merger of the Three Towns, Plymouth, Stonehouse and Devonport, it was decided to amalgamate Plymouth Tech with the slighter later Devonport Tech.

The latter still stands, but as residential accommodation, the former went in the mid-Sixties to make way for the new Drake Circus roundabout and the expanding new Technical College.

Opposite top: *The back of Drake Circus*. Bottom: *The Harvest Home (demolished on Sunday 29 November 1964)*. Top right: *Looking up Tavistock Road, past the Harvest Home to the old Tech, with the new Tech behind*. Bottom: *Close up of a similar view*.

There were many who didn't understand, or appreciate, the wholesale destruction of this area around the top end of Old Town Street and the beginning of Tavistock Road.

Compared with the rest of the commercial heart of the City there had been comparatively little wartime damage here, and now, more than 20 years after the Blitz - and even the end of the war - there were those who were reluctant to see time called on this Victorian quarter of the town.

The Harvest Home was by no means the only pub to be lost in this vicinity. In neighbouring Duke Street (which ran parallel to Pound Street), there were two more, the Revenue, on the corner of Tavistock Road, and the Sugar Refinery, on the corner of Saltash Street.

Both dated back to the middle of the nineteenth century and both bore names that spoke a little of the history of the area: the Revenue had originally, but not for long, been home to the local Inland Revenue Office, while the Sugar Refinery, which had opened as a butcher's shop, was named in honour of the Sugar Refinery that William Bryant and Edward James had set up in nearby Mill Lane, in 1838.

The actual refinery closed in 1886 but at one time, before they had sold out to the British and Irish Sugar Refining Company in 1856, the business had been paying about half of the customs receipts of the port of Plymouth.

Furthermore, in the early days of wireless broadcasting in Plymouth it seems that there was an aerial strung between the old chimneys of the Sugar Refinery that was linked by wire to the old BBC studios in Athenaeum Street.

There was no place for the sentimentalists though in the drive to complete the modern City Centre as Duke Street, Saltash Street, Compton Street, Clarence Street, parts of Park Street and Regent Street were all reduced to rubble.

In the post war period a number of the doomed buildings had been converted in a variety of ways and Plymouth's first coffee bar - the El Sombrero - had opened up in an empty unit opposite the Bedford Vaults pub at the top end of Old Town Street in 1957. The Tarantula and the Hideaway followed soon afterwards and the area enjoyed a brief era as the cool part of town for the city's younger generation.

Top left: Duke Street, with the Sugar Refinery pub on the left. Bottom: Looking along Regent Street from the bottom of Tavistock Place.

Looking up Saltash Street from its junction with Cornwall Street and Old Town Street.

However it was also much loved by the older generation too, for whom some of these buildings were reminders of their own youth.

At the dawn of the Fifties a large number of City Centre butchers were still to be found around the old market: Endacott, Andrews, Polkinghorne, Soper, Warren, Dewhurst, Bowden, Dingle, Martin, Strong, Deacon, Crabtree, Batstone, Ross, Merryfield, Parsons, and Mills.

In Market Avenue itself there were other businesses, among them the Leicester Shoe Company, a couple of bakers - Uglow's and Goodbody's - Coles, the tea and coffee importers, and Jeffery's sports' shop.

All of them destined to disappear as the decade progressed.

There was a similar tale to be told at the bottom end of Tavistock Road, the eastern section of which stood between the erstwhile Clarence Street and Park Street. This constituted, until 1961, a very small part of the main A38, running down into Old Town Street towards St Andrew's Cross.

The occupants of Clarence Chambers, with its impressive entrance, sandwiched between Sowden, Shaw and Smith estate agents, and Gertrude's wool shop, were counting down the days, as were the proprietors of Drake's tobacconists and confectioner and Clarke and Chinn's musical instrument store.

One or two of the shops already look as though they had been cleared out, including Gertrude's. One of many wool shops around town at the time, Gertrude also had a branch on Mutley Plain where you could buy a ball of wool for around 1/3d (6p) and knit yourself a reasonable size jumper for 10/- (50p) … and if you couldn't afford to buy all eight one-ounce balls at once, you could always put a batch back and buy them two at a time. Always best to put a batch back though, just in case the dyes didn't match when you next ordered!

Two views of buildings around the old Market taken shortly before their demolition.

Part of Tavistock Road, between Clarence Street (hence Clarence Chambers) and Park Street and running down into Old Town Street. This was then a very small section of the A38.

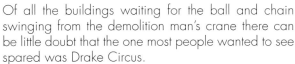

Of all the buildings waiting for the ball and chain swinging from the demolition man's crane there can be little doubt that the one most people wanted to see spared was Drake Circus.

Oddly enough this was one of the more modern parts of the pre-war city centre and was barely 40 years-old when the Luftwaffe launched their raids on Plymouth. Indeed, even as the 1960s dawned there would have been people around who could remember Old Town Street before the distinctively curved, but by no means circular, Circus was built. Furthermore most of those who were then in their mid-Thirties, or older, would certainly have known Drake Circus without its iconic clock.

However in a city where such illuminated advertising was rare, it was the Guinness Clock that made Drake Circus the striking feature that it was - had the non neon Bovril sign that had been there in the mid-Thirties remained, it is doubtful that the block would have been held quite so dear to the hearts of so many.

The local electrical contractors WG Heath had the sub-contract from the Electric Sign Company to service the clock and the strap lines.

'We had a back up for every letter in a little room behind the clock,' recalled Peter Coleman who worked for Heath's.

'The "Guinness Time" letters were all green and came on and stayed on, while the line underneath flashed.'

Just as generations had met by Derry's Clock, so many others had arranged a rendezvous or two underneath the Guinness Clock. Some even delighted in trying to walk in time to the flashing sign as one by one the words 'Guinness Is Good For You' flashed up.

From time to time there have been calls for its reinstatement over the years and Guinness nationally have re-introduced one or two, but generally only where the original building, or something similar, still stands.

This page and opposite: *Three early Sixties views of Drake Circus and Burton's Corner.*

Another major redevelopment that took place around the turn of the nineteenth into the twentieth century was the refashioning of Ebrington Street so that it could accommodate a tram route designed to run the length of Beaumont Road and service the Mount Gould estate.

The street, like Old Town Street itself, became wider and the buildings taller, and of course, newer. Once again this meant that there were but a few buildings here that were much more than 40 years old when the first bombs fell on Plymouth. But many of them fell within the designated zone of the new City Centre and so were inevitably denied the opportunity of living a full life and were cleared to make way for the new road down to Charles Church and to create a space upon which to build a much bigger Drake Circus than that which the city had previously known.

Moon's music store, Maypole's dairy, Jethro Ham the surgical boot maker, and Sanders & Son woodwork suppliers, were among those being forced out and made to think about relocation. The Co-op too had premises here, as did Amco radio suppliers, Bonny's draper's and Alan's fancy goods.

The bulldozers would head east as far as the Ham Street Vaults before drawing breath, and although that particular pub would see out the Sixties, it too was not long for this world.

Top: *Drake Circus with J&M Stone's electrical goods store far right and far left on the image on the opposite page.* Left: *Two atmospheric views of Old Town Street at night, with Burton's Corner on the right.*

The doomed western end of Ebrington Street c.1960

Drake Circus by day and night.

When the old Drake Circus building eventually fell prey to the crane, chain and ball, an attempt was made to rescue the Guinness clock and its attendant advertising. Sadly, according to one of the men involved, *'a lot of it was a bit on the rusty side and all the tubes had smashed. However, the two hands and the clock motor went into the WG Heath workshop and stayed there for a while.'* And there it remained until the boss ordered a clear out and it all ended up on the city tip at Chelson Meadow.

This page: *Peter Taylor's Sunday morning shots of the disappearing Drake Circus.*

The loss of Drake Circus and the subsequent construction of Charles Street virtually marked the end of an era. The new City Centre had been ring-road fenced: there were now only a handful of pre-war buildings inside the multi-laned roadway that now encircled the shopping centre. Punctuated by pedestrian subways, it was no longer possible, or at least advisable, to amble into town without dipping down into an artificially lit and not always inviting, tiled tunnel taking you under one or other of these busy vehicular routes.

As the Sixties came to an end and with the new Drake Circus still a year or two down the line, the planners had largely achieved their goal: the level of uniformity so relentlessly pursued at first had given way to a more laissez-faire, and certainly less appealing range of developments on the fringes of the centre, but at least it was shiny, bright and modern.

Plymouth now had the most state-of-the-art shopping centre in the whole of Britain.

How would it work? How would it stand the test of time? These were questions to which no-one could know the answers. Individuals might have their own ideas, but there was no crystal ball. The buildings that had been removed to make way for the plan had gone forever, it was too late to stop the process - it had been done.

There had been voices of dissent along the way, but there hadn't been a sufficient body of opinion to really influence matters.

However, the same could not be said about the situation on the Barbican.

Left: The new roundabout takes shape near the old Drake Circus site. 1966. Right top: Charles Church, preserved in the middle of another new roundabout as a memorial to the civilians who lost their lives in the City in the Second World War. Bottom: Charles Street under construction.

THE BARBICAN STORY

Like the rest of Plymouth, the Barbican had suffered from enemy bombing during the war, but not nearly as badly as the City Centre. Nevertheless there was talk of clearing much of what remained and creating a new community, albeit one that was dressed up as an historic precinct. The reality of the situation was that there was little intention of preserving much more than a handful of historic buildings. The local authority had begun a process of 'slum clearance' across the Barbican in the decade or so before the war and pressed ahead with this initiative in the decade or so after the war. Indeed our esteemed City Fathers oversaw the demolition of more Tudor and Jacobean properties in each of those pre and post-war periods than the Luftwaffe destroyed during the war.

The tragedy of this, of course, was that while most of what was lost to incendiaries and high explosives in the City Centre, was nineteenth century or later - indeed much of it was less than 50 years old at the time of the Blitz - the area now defined as the Barbican was effectively the full extent of the town prior to 1800.

There was an opportunity here to separate out the old part of the town and create a truly special historic precinct, but one by one old buildings were being lost to the developer and gradually more and more people started realise that their heritage was being plundered. Voices inside and outside the Council Chamber started to make themselves heard and it was clear that a crisis point had been reached when one Councillor suggested that it was time to replace the traditional Plymouth Crest of the saltire interspersed with the four towers of the town's medieval castle, with two bulldozers rampant. Ultimately, the straw that broke the proverbial camel's back was the demolition of the fine old Tudor hostelry - the Ring O'Bells.

Opposite page: *Barbican area in 1961 having lost many blitz survivors.*
Right: *Looking across Sutton Pool from the Fish Market.*

The Parade and the new block of flats facing Vauxhall Street, with a glimpse of the Georgian Exchange building far right. Opposite page: Two views of the old Ring of Bells.

The Ring of Bells had undoubtedly seen better days, but that was true of so many of the buildings in and around the Barbican, indeed that was the reason the local authorities wanted to pull so many of them down. Their stories had a common theme: once a grand property, home perhaps to some sixteenth century sea-captain or wealthy merchant, these houses had gradually gone down-market, and Plymouth's better off inhabitants had moved out of town as roads and transport improved, such that by the end of the nineteenth century they had almost invariably become rack-rented and neglected by greedy landlords.

The process of slum clearance had actually begun in Looe Street and How Street in the 1890s - hence the construction of the town's first municipal flats in those streets. In the Twenties and Thirties the practice continued, most notably in High Street, and after the war the government's decision to award a new building licence for every old building destroyed, only served to encourage the process.

However Plymouth was rapidly running low on its stock of really old buildings and the historic heart of the City was in grave danger of becoming a post-war housing estate, made up almost entirely of flats, punctuated only by the odd historic building, much like post-war Devonport, only there the buildings - like Foulston's 1820's classically themed group around the top of Ker Street - were not quite as old.

Conservation was not an entirely novel concept, but it had few champions in the early Fifties. Fortunately, however, the destruction of the Ring of Bells, a building that still boasted most of its original Tudor features inside, stirred a few disparate groups and individuals into action. There had, evidently, been plans to list the property, but the demolition men moved in before it could be saved.

Time had been called ... time for action.

Top: *John Macgregor addresses the Old Plymouth Society in Abbey Hall.* Above: *Jim Woodrow and Hilary Cornish lead dignitaries on a tour of the Barbican.*

Here and there people got together, meetings were held - one of the first was in the relatively newly opened Arts Centre at the top of Looe Street. Arthur Southcombe Parker, who had been largely responsible for setting up the Old Plymouth Society and saving 32 New Street (the Elizabethan House) in the late-Twenties, once again dusted off his activist's hat. Lady Astor's support was sought and given. Sir John Betjeman lent his voice to the campaign, and, most significantly of all, a group of young professionals, all of them local men, most of them war veterans, still only in their thirties, took charge of the situation. They formed an offshoot of the Old Plymouth Society - the Plymouth Barbican Association.

The newly formed body managed to enlist the help and support of two councillors, one from either side – Stanley Goodman and Leslie Paul.

'We found out that a house that was unfit need not be demolished as long as it was not used as living accommodation. The Council offered to lease to us for 999 years, six adjoining houses in New Street - but, we had to find guarantors for £100,000 ... and we did.' Founder member Peter Stedman writing in the foreword to *Plymouth's Historic Barbican* (2007).

'Four stalwarts each pledged £25,000; Jimmy Woodrow (of steel fabricators Blight and White), CP Brown (of Brown, Wills and Nicholson), Humphrey Woolcombe (solicitor) and Gerald Whitmarsh (accountant). It was an important moment.'

It was indeed, £5,000 would have bought you a very reasonable property in 1957, so it was a huge sum to underwrite, but it meant that the Plymouth Barbican Association was up and running and over the next ten years or so they would kick start the transformation of the Barbican from a run-down area with seemingly little to commend it, to a popular tourist centre, populated by arts and craftsmen, antique markets and second-hand bookshops, old pubs, clubs, bars, and cafes, and new restaurants in ancient buildings.

Looe Street and New Street came first and before long the Barbican Association had restored a handful of Tudor and Jacobean properties in the former and half a dozen or so in the latter.

With additional properties in Stokes Lane, the Parade and the Barbican itself, the Association quickly built up an enviable portfolio of buildings, almost all of which had been earmarked for demolition.

It also meant, in terms of conservation, that Plymouth was well ahead of the game.

Above: 4 June 1964, formal opening of the renovated 33 Looe Street, l-r; The Earl of Mount Edgcumbe, Lord Mayor, Tom Watkins, Peter Stedman, Humphrey Woollcombe, Hilary Cornish, Stanley Edgcumbe, Arthur Marshman and Walton Gale. Right: Two views of New Street.

One of the relatively few bomb sites on the Barbican - before the war here had been the Mayflower Hotel

Where the Barbican Association led, others followed, and gradually more and more buildings were opened up as the Barbican became an increasingly fertile area for anyone thinking of starting up a small business. Eventually the wider Plymouth population overcame any earlier prejudices they had about the Barbican and tourists simply took the place at face value and voted with their feet. With a street pattern that Drake would have recognised, the largest concentration of cobbled streeting in England and over 100 listed buildings, the area became a natural magnet for visitors.

Initially it would appear, though, that despite the great steps forward being taken with regard to conservation, the local authorities weren't overly concerned about the design or quality of the new buildings proposed for the area's bomb sites. Certainly the new restaurant that appeared on the sensitive site by the Mayflower memorial appeared to have little or no empathy with any of its neighbours.

Above: *The first new build on the Barbican since the war - Ristoranti Capri - as it was originally known.*

Above: *Early morning on the Barbican.* Far left: *The Admiral MacBride.* Left: *Island House and the Crown and Anchor.*

A significant element in the Barbican's appeal to the artisan and artist, was the number of old pubs that populated the area. The Ring of Bells hadn't been open since sometime before the war, but there were literally dozens of others, and as the predominantly nineteenth-century city centre pubs were being lost in the redevelopment, so the older Barbican hostelries in the very heart of old Plymouth, became increasingly attractive.

Along the Barbican itself we had: the Admiral MacBride (named after the Plymouth MP who had secured the construction of the east and west piers in the late-eighteenth century), the Crown and Anchor (renamed the Sir Francis Chichester in 1967) and the Dolphin (a favourite haunt of the Hoe guest house landlady who would become an internationally famous artist in the Seventies - Beryl Cook).

In Southside Street there were the Navy, the Maritime and the Queens Arms - a good example of a sympathetic new development built in the mid-Sixties on the site of a blitzed sixteenth-century pub.

In 1961, with the encouragement of the Civic Trust, the Barbican Association, in partnership with the City Council, carried out an improvement scheme for Southside Street. The initiative saw street lighting moved to brackets on buildings, the general tidying up and improvement of street furniture and a painting scheme devised for the whole street that was designed to give special attention to the colour washes and the lettering of signs.

Such was the scale of the transformation that the Barbican was now deemed to be fit for a queen and the following year Queen Elizabeth II did something her predecessor could have done, but never did, on account of the fact that she never ventured this far west - she walked along New Street and Southside Street, just as Sir Francis Drake may have done a hundred times or more.

Top right: Southside Street in 1966. Right: Southside Street in 1961. Far right: The Queen's Arms - completed and opened in 1966.

Above: *Barbican Fish Market.* Left: *Work inside the Fish Market.*

The Queen's Barbican tour inevitably took her past the Fish Market, which, at that point in time, was somewhat in decline and had been since the end of the war. The fishing industry had been a core source of employment and revenue for the area for the best part of a thousand years, but by 1963 there were only eight large boats fishing out of Sutton Harbour. However, thanks largely to the extension of British territorial waters in 1967 - from three miles to twelve - the situation improved substantially - and the following year saw the local catch increase by 50% (to 12,500 cwt with a value of £82,000) and the number of first-class boats working out of the port rose to 14. Notwithstanding those figures, however, Brixham and Newlyn, both formerly smaller than Plymouth in terms of the trade, managed to substantially overtake the operations here. Nevertheless it was good news and Sutton Harbour invested £25,000 on improving the fish market services and Bigwoods (Plymouth Cold Store Limited), local ice merchants since 1789, installed a new ice plant in a building constructed for the purpose by Sutton Harbour, who also erected a new range of offices.

Top left: *The Island House and entrance to the Fish Market.* Top right: *Her Majesty the Queen walks through the Barbican in July 1962.* Bottom right: *Fishing boats alongside the Market.*

North Quay, Sutton Harbour from Marrowbone Slip.

Sutton Harbour was, throughout this time, still very much a working harbour. In addition to the wet fish returns there was also a substantial shellfish trade, worth an additional £23,500 in 1968.

Beyond the fish market itself, the quays of the harbour were lined with warehouses and workplaces. The Co-op had rebuilt their large warehouse on North Quay in 1950, but apart from that there was precious little in the way of new construction on the northern or eastern sides of Sutton Harbour. But all this would change. The rail link to North Quay and Coxside had gone and that was bound to impact on what could and couldn't be done around the waterfront.

Shipbuilding had long since been replaced by ship breaking, but even that wasn't destined to be a long-term role for the area. Demellweek and Redding were the firm responsible, most notably, for breaking up the fondly remembered Great Western Tender, Sir Francis Drake, here in 1954 and, three years later, the celebrated HMS Amethyst, of the July 1950 Yangtse Incident fame (when the British Embassy guardship was caught up in the middle of the Chinese Civil War) met a similar fate on Marrowbone Slip.

Top right: *The Cooperage and the Co-op warehouse, North Quay.* Above: *North Quay from Fish Market.*

A view across Sutton Harbour of the Prince Rock Power Station and Coxside Gas Works.

Generally, however, work around the harbour was gradually drying up. Before the war, the amount of material imported into the Sutton Pool annually was on a par with the activity in MIllbay, nudging around the quarter of a million tons mark. The figures dwindled during the Second World War, but by 1950 had picked up again and just broke the 200,000 ton mark, but the trade was heavily dependent on the coal and coke market - with a little bit of timber trade..

Coal was still a significant power generator at that time and in 1960 Sutton Harbour handled 162,000 of the 266,000 tons of coal shipped into the city - it also accounted for over 12,000 tons of the port's exports (roughly 15%), most of which was coke and spent oxide.

The body blow to this trade however came in 1969 when the South Western Gas Board closed its coal-burning gas works at Coxside which, overnight, wiped 100,000 tons off Sutton Harbour's annual imports and 10,000 tons of its export quota. Effectively this meant that Sutton Harbour's life as a commercial shipping base was - apart from the fishing - in terminal decline.

Top left: *HMS Amethyst being broken up on Marrowbone Slip.* Top right: *German cargo ship Luhe Stade in Sutton Harbour.* Bottom: *All is still in the busy, little, industrial Sutton Pool.*

The Plymouth Belle picks up passengers from the Mayflower Steps on West Pier, with timber yards and the coal depot in the distance..

A bit of coal and a little fertiliser trade were soon all that was left of the import market, while the export trade was virtually confined to steel turnings. But there was no great volume and it was clear that if the harbour was going to remain viable it would have to look for other openings.

The leisure and pleasure industry was starting to show signs of greater interest in water sports, but there were not yet sufficient levels of disposable income or readily affordable dinghies to make much of an impact. However, given the huge amount of progress made in making the Barbican a more welcoming spot for visitors, from home and abroad, it soon became apparent that there might be a good opportunity to try to court the growing local tourist market.

Pleasure boats had been plying their trade from Phoenix Wharf since the nineteenth century, and there had been a stone inscribed with the legend 'Mayflower 1620', on a site near to where the Pilgrim Fathers last stood on English soil before setting off for the brave new world, since 1890. Now, once again through the good offices of the Barbican Association, a plaque was erected on the wall of the Island House listing the names of all the passengers who had sailed on that historic ship (although initially it only named the male passengers).

A replica of the *Mayflower* sailed into Plymouth Sound in 1957 and a decade later, an old Baltic trawler, converted to look like Drake's *Golden Hind* (it was later renamed the *Hispaniola*), drew good crowds. The real jewel in the crown, though, was still the Hoe.

Far right: *Two views of the old Baltic trawler, converted to pass itself off as the* Hispaniola, *moored alongside West Pier.* Right: *The list of Pilgrim Fathers on the wall of the Island House.*

Above: Parking on one side only, but it's two-way traffic around the front of Plymouth Hoe. Opposite page: Boehm's statue of Drake on the Hoe Promenade.

ON THE HOE

Plymouth Hoe had first been laid out as a formal public open park, with a lodge, cafe, and memorials in the 1880s.

In a momentous ten-year period Smeaton's 120-year-old lighthouse was dismantled, block by block and brought back to the mainland and erected less than a mile from where it had been fashioned, on the edge of Millbay (there was nothing wrong with the structure itself, but there were fears over the reef upon which it had been built, hence the need to replace it). Two years later, in February 1884, a replica of Boehm's statue of Sir Francis Drake in Tavistock, was unveiled on the Promenade; three months after that the first phase of Plymouth Pier was opened (it was one of the first buildings in Plymouth to be *'lighted by electricity'*); then, in 1888, the Armada Tercentenary Memorial was unveiled and, to conclude the decade of decoration, in 1891, the year the pier was completed, the colonnaded Belvedere, that sat directly behind the pier entrance, was erected.

The Hoe park's reputation as a popular place to promenade was thus sealed in that period (it had been used as grazing land for cows and sheep before that) and, apart from the loss of the pier to enemy incendiaries, and the metal bandstand to the war effort, the Hoe had escaped the ravages of war relatively lightly. Not only, therefore, was it well placed to pick up where it had left off before the war, but it could consolidate its position as a rallying point for the city, for throughout the war, the Astors had led dances on the Hoe. Invoking the defiant spirit of Drake, they moved to the music of live bands under the would-be reassuring shadow of a barrage balloon.

Lord Astor (who served the city as an a-political Lord Mayor for most of the war) had died in 1952 and Lady Nancy Astor, who died twelve years later, bequeathed their Plymouth home - No.3 Elliot Terrace, overlooking the Promenade, to the City, complete with all its fixtures and fittings.

East Hoe, the Royal Plymouth Corinthian Yacht Club, the Royal Citadel and the Aquarium from Smeaton's Tower.

Of course the post-war layout of the City that cut a great green swathe from the railway station to the Hoe right through the City Centre, made access easier than ever. However, as the motor car become more and more affordable, many who might formerly have spent a day or an afternoon on the Hoe, took the option to explore the wider surroundings. Consequently, while still busy, numbers on the Hoe never quite reached the pre-war peaks of popularity - apart from the high days and holidays when some special event, on the Hoe or in the Sound, might induce great crowds up onto the high ridge, the 'Haw', from whence it derives it's name.

Nevertheless on a sunny day the two-way route around the front of the Citadel - a route that had only opened in the 1930s - was invariably lined with cars, parked freely on the edge of the pavement, the driver and passengers not worrying about how long they could stay.

The sun terraces and the highly sought after wooden beach huts would be full.

Equipped with lockers, tables and chairs, the huts were available for day use only at Tinside, Pebbleside and Hoe foreshore. Generally booked by the week (Sunday to Saturday) the cost varied according to the time of year. Anyone wanting to just hire a hut for a day, on the day, had to take pot luck. You couldn't book in advance and if they were already all taken, then that was it.

Further around, towards the Royal Plymouth Corinthian Yacht Club, there was the mysterious Lion's Den. With it's curved wall and glazed roof, this facility was available for all those men, young and old, who were happy to go for an all-over tan … and certainly not even considering the possibility that someone might be watching from Mount Batten with a very powerful telephoto lens on their camera.

On the top of the Hoe, in the lee of the Citadel walls, the Marine Biological Association harboured Plymouth's Aquarium, which, it was said, 'is of modern construction and one of the finest in Europe. 'Attractive underwater scenes display exceptionally well a large variety of local sea-fishes and other marine animals.'

Remarkably the aquarium was open until 8pm in the summer season and 10am to 6pm from October through to April.

Opening hours generally were more generous than today. In 1965 Tinside Pool was open all year round, from 7am in the summer and from 9am in the winter (the same timings applied to the pools at Mount Wise too).

Above: *The Hoe chalets, cafe and Smeaton's Tower.* Inset: *The MBA's Aquarium.*

The Lion's Den, rafts and Tinside Pool, looking across West Hoe to the grain silo at Millbay.

Predictably the busiest times on the Hoe came during the summer holidays and among the many inducements run by Frank Bottom, Plymouth's Entertainments and Publicity Manager, were: a Happy Child contest for children aged between 6 and 10 - held every Friday from the end of July to the end of August; a Junior Miss, for girls of ages between 10 and 15, staged at the same time: and on 'Swimmers' Day' at Tinside pool there was an annual Bathing Belle and an annual Mr Plymouth Contest. In 1965 this was held on Wednesday 18 August at 2.30pm, while a fortnight later, at 2.45pm, in the Hoe Theatre, there was a Fashion Queen contest, which like the Bathing Belle affair was for 'ladies of any age over 16' - there appeared to be no age restrictions, incidentally, for the Mr Plymouth event.

Mind you, within a year or two there was no Mr Plymouth event, and by 1968 the Bathing Belle contest had also been dropped from the summer schedules.

Busy as Tinside Lido was, there were always other options, and for those who didn't feel they needed to lock up their valuables in the changing rooms, there was always a free swim out to the rafts or in one of the side pools west of Tinside.

The diving board was another attraction for those brave, or foolhardy, enough to have a go.

Above: *Bathing beauties at Tinside.* Right: *Two views of Tinside.*

Looking across Armada Way from the Civic Centre towards the Hoe and Plymouth Sound.

Hot drinks and pasties were ever among the refreshments on offer and in 1965 the delights of the Hoe Cafe were supplemented by the construction of the Mallard Cafe above Tinside.

The Hoe Cafe itself had arrived on the Hoe in 1947: a former aircraft hangar from the World War II RAF base at Yelverton (Harrowbeer) it was erected on the site of the 1920s Hoe Pavilion which had been destroyed during the war.

Interestingly enough, the opening of the Mallard didn't mean the end of the 'blimp' as it was affectionately known, and both structures served visitors to the Hoe throughout the Sixties and Seventies.

The Hoe Park and more especially the link to it, Armada Way, was still evolving as the Sixties progressed. It's worth remembering that Citadel Road had run right through the area at the back of the War Memorial before the war, and for many years after hostilities had ended.

Gradually, however, the great wide boulevard was created, the last few obstructions were removed and new buildings were planned for fringes of the widest stretch just below Citadel Road. At the end of the decade proposals were submitted for the city's tallest hotel - the Holiday Inn - which like the similarly proportioned Mayflower Hotel, beyond the Millbay end of the Hoe Promenade, would open in time for the Mayflower 350th Anniversary celebrations in 1970.

The full peripheral tidying up exercise would take much longer and a number of pre-war survivors clung on to give Armada Way a ragged western edge below the Hoe.

Essentially though, the great green open space that generations had known before the war, grew even greater.

'The Hoe is Plymouth's sea-front park,' said the guide books, 'where hundreds of people - from courting couples to family groups - gather for a happy time.'

Top: *Looking back down Armada Way c.1961*. Bottom: *The doomed properties in Citadel Road.*

The Mallard Cafe was built on a hitherto vacant garden plot just below the old watchtower. This curious little octagonal edifice had been built sometime around 1870 for the benefit of shipping firms, who, in the days before radio communications, could watch from here for mail steamers making their way towards the Sound, so that arrangements could be made, as soon as possible, for tenders to be made ready to meet the boats and whisk the postbags and important passengers on to waiting trains at Millbay.

Millbay Station, of course, had closed to passenger traffic during the war, but over at West Hoe there was the perennially popular mini-railway. Located inside a brightly coloured picket-fence the sixpenny rides on the Thomas the Tank-style engines provided countless photographic opportunities for visitors and locals alike.

Meanwhile, the situation further around the waterfront, beyond Rusty Anchor at Millbay, was, like that in Sutton Harbour, suffering from a number of commercial crises.

Above and top left: The site of the Mallard Cafe. Bottom left: The Mallard does good business as the crowds await the return of Sir Francis Chichester.

West Hoe play park - various views.

Millbay and West Hoe, 1968. Opposite page: A tranquil scene at Millbay Docks

MILLBAY DOCKS AND STONEHOUSE CREEK

The port of Plymouth's principal commercial docks were at Millbay. Set up by Brunel as the Great Western Docks in the 1840s and serviced by the neighbouring railway station that opened at the end of that decade, the docks prospered for the best part of 100 years. Enemy bombing curtailed the passenger services in and out of Millbay, in 1941, but the goods trains kept running and operated all through the 1960s. The situation there, however, was far from being rosy.

In 1961 the visit of the famous French liner, Liberte, marked the virtual end of a long and colourful history of Millbay as a liner port of call and spelt the end of the working lives of two much-loved tenders - the Sir John Hawkins and Sir Richard Grenville. The former was withdrawn from service in 1962, the latter, a year later (a third tender, the Sir Francis Drake, had been scrapped in the Fifties and a fourth, the Sir Walter Raleigh, in the Forties).

Millbay Docks c.1960 showing various vessels: Eddy Bay (in the dry dock) and in the inner basin: RFA Robert Dundas (a coastal stores carrier launched in 1938), RFA Green Ranger (a fleet support tanker, ordered in 1939 and wrecked off the Hartland Peninsula in 1962), RV Sarsia (built in 1953 as a fisheries research vessel and belonging to the National Oceanography Centre), Scott Discovery, The Queen (Coal Ship) and Williams Tug.

The Docks were, nevertheless, still home to a number of shipping agents - Cory & Strick, Bellamy & Co., Weekes, Phillips & Co., Fox & Sons, Orlando Davis - and the local ship repairers and marine engineers Willoughby's.

Established in 1844 as the docks were being developed, Willoughby's were established in and around the dry dock at Millbay and over the years merged with or acquired one or two other foundries, until, following the union with Bickle & Co in 1958, they were the only major engineering firm left around the harbour. With a workforce of around 150 the future didn't look all that bleak, however, in 1969, with no money available for the dry dock to be repaired, a decision was taken to close the business and plans were put in motion to infill the dock and pave the way for the arrival of a roll-on, roll-off ferry service to France. Millbay had been handling imports from Brittany for many years - strawberries, green vegetables and potatoes were regularly shipped across from Plougastel between January and June every year and then whisked off to places like Cardiff, Birmingham, Sheffield, Manchester, Edinburgh and London overnight.

Publicity for Millbay at the time informed us that the bulk of these goods were carried by *'rail, trucks being despatched almost as soon as loading is completed. The fruit is imported in flimsy wooden crates of about 12lbs weight which are loaded in the hold onto wooden pallets, discharged by crane and loaded into "Fruit D" trucks, the usual samples being taken for Customs examination. The trucks are lightly loaded to avoid crushing.'*

Cargo handling facilities at Millbay had been up-graded in the Fifties and Sixties, and grain was landed here at the imposing West Wharf silo, while coal was landed at South Quay for the Co-op. Animal feed, farm machinery, lager, bacon, salt and paper were among the other imports, and Clyde Quay and Glasgow Quay were also busy. At the height of the potato season loads of up to 2,000 tons would be discharged *'non-stop from arrival to completion.'*

However as the Sixties progressed so the trade slackened. There was little use for Clyde or Glasgow Quay after 1966 and with the closure of Millbay Station in 1971 the port's future looked increasingly uncertain. A few larger trawlers started landing fish here, but Millbay had lost a lot of its buzz. Only the occasional use of the facilities as a rallying point for transatlantic racing yachts brought any real colour to the area.

Right: Millbay Docks in use as a racing yacht haven as well as a working docks.

Stonehouse Creek looking across to the Rectory, Tamar School and Devonport High School for Boys.

Further around the waterfront there were changes afoot in the nature of the work being carried out on either side of Stonehouse Creek.

The creek, then, still extended as far as the old Millbridge (it had reached as far as Pennycomequick prior to the construction of Victoria Park at the turn of the century). Furthermore, until the mid-Sixties trains were still operating in and out of King's Road Station and Ocean Quay Terminal at Richmond Walk, but the former closed to passengers in 1964, and to all rail traffic seven years later, while the latter, which had been operating as a goods only service for many years, closed in 1966.

With the electricity station at Stonehouse long gone and the independent breweries disappearing, there was little in the way of long-standing enterprises still around, although there were Penny's coal merchants and a couple of scrap metal men - Basil Totterdale and Percy Windsor. Meanwhile Monsen's and Saccone & Speed had bonded stores in Newport Street and in 1964 the old Sulphuro Fertilizers premises was transformed into a waste paper converting business. That same summer saw another infant company appear, Marine Projects, which, like it's neighbour, was destined for great things.

Above: *Newport Street, Stonehouse.*

Top: *Stonehouse Creek and the Rectory.* Bottom: *Further down the creek.* Inset: *Peter Attrill and his boat in the summer of 1963 with Newport Street behind him.*

The Royal William Yard from Mount Wise.

DEVONPORT

The gradual escalation in the number and popularity of small yachts and sailing dinghies occasioned one of the more subtle changes to the local waterfront across the Sixties and it was accompanied by a gradual decline in the amount of commercial and naval shipping coming in and out of the Sound.

The passing of the Cold War saw a reduction in defence spending and led to a general contraction in the armed services and the very raison d'être for Devonport. And, in a very different way, the construction of the indoor swimming pool meant that there was less demand for the pools at Mount Wise - the scene of many a happy school swimming gala. All in all the situation in Devonport was not great: the once-proud Georgian town had been in decline since the Amalgamation of the Three Towns - Plymouth, Stonehouse and Devonport - in 1914. After the First World War Devonport still had it's own department stores, cinemas, theatres and churches … but many of these had been lost or damaged during the war and there was little or no attempt to replace them.

Above: *New Pier Inn, Mutton Cove.* Right: *Views of and from Mount Wise Swimming Baths.*

With improved transport links and greater car ownership there seemed to be an underlying feeling that it didn't matter about replacing these facilities in Devonport: the fact that the Three Towns were now one big city - Plymouth - the third biggest city south of Birmingham, meant that as long as these facilities were replaced somewhere in the city, all would be fine. And clearly, what Devonport needed, more than anything else was new housing.

There had been agonising delays in making certain decisions on account of the Admiralty's prevarication over just how much of pre-war Devonport they wanted to swallow up with their extension to South Yard. In the event their lordships' land-grab successfully cut the community in half and two new local hubs were created: one around Marlborough Street to the north; the other around Ker Street to the south.

An ugly, uninspiring stone wall, capped with barbed wire, created an oppressive space either side of the divide.

Ron Johns' parents had a shop near the Brown Bear: *'When the wall went up trade dropped about 75% overnight. The business was restyled as a coffee bar – with the Beatles a permanent fixture on the jukebox. Soon afterwards it became a late-licence night club – Rovaro's.'* However even that wasn't enough to keep the business afloat and before long Rovaro's relocated to the Barbican and became Ronnie's.

Left: *View from Devonport Column across Pembroke Street to Mount Wise, the Royal William Yard and Plymouth Sound.* Above: *Chapel Street, Devonport, 9 December 1966.*

The Brown Bear had been a rare survivor along with around 20 others of the 100 or so pubs that had been in Devonport 50 years earlier. Many had closed as the Dockyard had declined, yet others had been lost during the war, but many more were lost in the redevelopment, among them; Duke Street Inn, Bakers Arms, Foresters Arms (Duke Street), the Impregnable (James Street), the Albion, Rose and Crown, Himalaya (Pembroke Street), the White Swan (George Street), the Volunteer (Chapel Street), the Duke of Wellington, Morice Town Vaults, Royal Alfred, Royal Standard and Steam Reserve (William Street).

The old pubs weren't the only casualties though, as a number of other impressive period pieces were sacrificed, most notably, after a valiant campaign to keep them supported by Stanley Goodman and the old Plymouth Society, the fine Foulston terrace that stood just down from his group of Georgian classics - the Town Hall, Column and Egyptian building. Happily they survived, but piece by piece most of old Devonport was removed and the area became dominated by tower blocks, flats and other bland developments.

Top: *The new flats at the junction of Ker Street and Duke Street, across from the Old Chapel pub.* Bottom: *A spirited campaign championed by the Old Plymouth Society couldn't save the Foulston houses on the south side of Ker Street.*

February 1963 saw the opening of the new Naval Stores Building in South Yard - note the old houses in the foreground, most of which were not long for this world.

When earlier residential properties did survive it was generally where the buildings were comparatively new, like the three-storey 1930s flats that lined either side of Cornwall Street leading down to Cornwall Beach. Duke Street, Mount Street, Clowance Street and Prospect Row, also largely survived the cull.

However, further signs of a community that was rapidly disintegrating came when the decision was taken that the ecclesiastical needs of the area could be met by merging the parishes of St Stephen's, St Paul's, St John the Baptist and St Mary's under one roof - that of St Aubyn's in Chapel Street. The Reverend JH Jones was appointed to look after the united congregation. Meanwhile the other churches, some of which, like St John and St Mary, had survived the war, the latter, unscathed, were demolished in 1959.

Youth clubs, at this time, were seen as important social centres and there were several dotted around South Devonport – the Dockland Settlement at Bluff Battery, the Johnston Memorial Hall in Clowance Lane: there were meetings here every evening as well as being the base for Devonport Amateur Boxing Club. There were also Youth Club meetings three evenings a week at Methodist Central Hall – the Welcome – in Fore Street, plus scout and guide evenings.

In addition to these social centres the old Guildhall in Ker Street, which was now owned by the Corporation, was used as a Folk Club.

Top left: Looking up Cornwall Street. Bottom: Looking down towards Cornwall Beach before the bridge was erected between South Yard and Morice Yard in 1967. Above: A bus passes Granby flats at the top of Park Avenue.

Meanwhile, the Forum Cinema had been converted to a Bingo Hall and a 'teenage' dance hall known briefly as the Key Club. The club had moved across from the Barbican and opened with top rhythm and blues band Georgie Fame and the Blue Flames. Later, mod-rockers, the Who, played there. All in all, however, the Key club era lasted less than a year, and the club moved on to the Purple Fez in Exmouth Road. Other facilities, also existed, like the Fleet Club, and the Salvation Army Red Shield Club at Granby Way, but were mainly used by service personnel.

That too was an ever diminishing number and with the demolition of Raglan and Granby Barracks it was clear that there was another era that had now vanished, almost without trace.

In their stead we now had regimental blocks of domestic accommodation, much of it not desperately family-friendly. As the authors of the 1966 City of Plymouth: South Devonport Report put it, *'It will be noted that no further one-bedroom and bed-sitting accommodation is proposed for the area.'*

However the proliferation of single person units wasn't the only obstacle to family friendly housing: *'Probably the most significant factor requiring a fresh examination of the Marlborough Street area has been the change of opinion arising from greater experience of the social and economic consequences of very high-density housing schemes.*

'Broadly it can be said that not only is the cost of high-density building very high per dwelling, but it provides accommodation in a form which is not generally desired by the majority of families which Councils have to house.' The report continued: *'There is little doubt that flats, especially in high blocks, are far from ideal for families with children, particularly young children.'* Utilitarian and flat, they were surrounded by little in the way of greenery or play spaces.

Left: *The Queen and Constitution, James Street.* Above: *Devonport's three new tower blocks.*

The Royal Albert Gate with the remains of William Street on the far left.

Another major issue for the planners was that of parking spaces. Consequently, among the various proposals put forward in a 1964 Marlborough Street area report there were plans for a four-storey car park, adjoining South Yard Gate, for around 240 vehicles to be built by the Ministry of Defence (which now incorporated the Admiralty); accommodation for 96 cars on the west side of Marlborough Street and abutting the east side of an improved Morice Street, plus a further 30 spaces along New Passage Hill and garage accommodation for 253 cars (one per dwelling) for the proposed residential development.

New Passage Hill, by this time, had been recently eclipsed by Park Avenue, a new route that had first been recommended at the dawn of the Fifties by the City Engineer James Paton Watson. Road traffic between the wars had multiplied ten-fold and business traffic since 1938 had doubled (by 1951) - Paton Watson had therefore proposed a major new road from the top of Chapel Street through Granby Barracks across Devonport Park, and along Garden Street, into Albert Road.

In the event it wasn't until 1957 that the Barracks were removed, along with the barrack wall in Princess Street, and construction of the road became possible. Meanwhile the road that had previously been the principal route between the entrance to Keyham Steam Yard and the heart of old Devonport - William Street - was all but annihilated, along with Mooncove Street and much of Charlotte Street, as the long hand of the Admiralty again reached out and appropriated a significant amount of land, this time at the bottom end of Albert Road.

Work begins on the new road through Devonport Park.

Above: *North Yard.* Inset: *Navy Days programmes from 1961 and 1966.*

However, as might be surmised from the Admiralty's prevarication over the extent of the Dockyard expansion, work at Devonport after the war was not as abundant as it might have been. With the conclusion of hostilities the order for the aircraft carrier, *Polyphemus*, was cancelled as was the completion of the patrol boats *Ace* and *Achetes* after their launches in March and September 1945.

It wasn't until June 1953 that a new warship was built at Devonport: a new air-type direction frigate, the *Salisbury*, was the first all-welded vessel to be put together in the Yard. Six years later *HMS Plymouth* slid into the Hamoaze and was followed by *Tartar* in 1960, *Cleopatra* in 1964, *Danae* in 1965 and *Scylla* in 1968. Six frigates in 15 years – a stark contrast to the first 14 years of the twentieth century when the Dockyard had turned out ten battleships, two battle cruisers and three cruisers.

The situation was not destined to improve either, as the *Scylla* was the last warship to be built at Devonport.

Such is not to suggest, though, that work in the Yard dried up altogether, indeed whilst there was not enough to sustain the immediate post-war peak of 21,000 dockyard workers, Devonport became a major centre for the conversion into and refitting of, aircraft carriers. *Furious*, *Glorious*, *Courageous* and *Hermes* were all big conversion jobs, while the *Eagle* and the *Ark Royal* were regularly in for refits, the former arriving for a four-year 'modernisation' in 1960 – the project costing £30 million and employing 3,000 men, and the latter also undergoing a £30 million refit from 1966 to 1969.

Of course it wasn't just the ships that were undergoing modernisation, the Dockyard itself was undergoing major changes. New Central Offices were built on part of the William Street site between 1964 and 1966 and, as part of the restructuring, the building of a wall around this new extension was taken as an opportunity to move the gate to Keyham Yard from the bottom of Albert Road and the Dockyard clock was moved from one western tower into the one nearer the road.

Around the same time an overhead road link was established between this new part of the Yard and Morice Yard and between Morice Yard and South Yard. Vehicles no longer needed to go out of the Yard to get from one part to another and thus the internal transport situation was hugely improved. The demise of the old Dockyard train was hastened by these developments, thereby drawing a line

Top: The Ark Royal returns. Bottom: An historic day: 8 August 1968 – the last warship to be built in Devonport – HMS Scylla – is launched.

Top: *March 1963, the last Dockyard train.* Above: *King's Road Station (Bernard Mills).*

under a system that had served the yard one way or another for over 100 years, and which at its height had some 20 miles of track in constant use. At one time or another some 70 locomotives had been employed on the internal railway – a railway that had links to the national network and, underground, between all three yards.

Up until its closure the system had also provided a free passenger service throughout the Yard, across the whole of the twentieth century, and had boasted six classes of accommodation from general labourer through to Principal Officers and the Admiral.

A restricted rail service, for the transportation of goods, continued to operate for some years, but the passenger service was replaced by coaches initially, and then, from December 1969, by six double-decker buses (four for Dockyardies and two for naval ratings).

The changes weren't confined to the physical environment either. In October 1966 a new post was created – General Manager for Devonport Dockyard: 54-year-old Captain Horace Gerald Southwood was appointed and tasked with forming a new management structure, similar to that recently implemented in the three other Royal Dockyards.

Southwood's period of tenure also saw a commitment expressed in 1968–69 to modernise and redevelop Devonport: the Dockyard henceforth became a base for Type 21 and 22 frigates. At the same time the Navy Minister, Dr David Owen, who was then the MP for Plymouth Sutton, announced that Devonport was to become an operational base for nuclear submarines and for the docking, refitting and refuelling of said submarines.

And, as has already been noted, the demise of the old technologies was by no means confined to the Dockyard. Steam trains were on their way out nationally, and so too were a lot of the lines they had travelled on. The passenger service to King's Road Station ended on 7 September 1964, along with the link between St Budeaux (Victoria Road) and Devonport Junction. Seven years later the last goods train pulled out of King's Road and the station closed altogether. Of course these closures were not exclusive to Devonport as Dr Beeching's axe cut rail services right across the country. Some 3,000 (roughly half) of all British stations (and around a quarter of the rail routes) were lost in the ten years following the publication of Richard Beeching's report *The Reshaping of British Railways*.

The intention was to stem the losses incurred in the wake of the expansion of road transport and business and private vehicular traffic. Only viable stations and routes were kept and clearly King's Road was not deemed to be one of them.

Opposite page: *1964, summer, the 11.47am Exeter Central to Plymouth via Okehampton.* Inset: *8 March 1968, the Duke of Edinburgh passes though on his way to open the Maritime College (Bernard Mills).*

Before long the station would disappear altogether and the site would be transformed as the city's newest educational facility - Plymouth College of Further Education - would appear in its stead.

Meanwhile in an unrelated, but adjacent, development the tidal creek just south of the station was filled in the year after King's Road closed. Actually the events weren't entirely unrelated as much of the infill material came from redundant British Rail buildings and bridges (some came from the Dockyard as it was being redeveloped too). This removed a 'stinking mud flats' situation and afforded extra sporting facilities for the schools – Devonport High School for Boys and Tamar – that had moved into neighbouring blocks of the old Military Hospital in the 1940s.

The imposing Devonport Technical College meanwhile had joined with Plymouth Tech in 1914 and as the twentieth century put further demands on higher technical and practical education so the college expanded and became the Plymouth College of Technology in 1962. The Tech, however, would soon enough become an annexe of the new College of Further Education, and a new generation would come to enjoy the delights of Devonport Park as a lunchtime retreat or a venue for a bit of fresh air and maybe a game of tennis.

Top: *Devonport Technical College.* Above left: *Ocean Quay terminal October 1965 (Bernard Mills).* Right: *Stonehouse Pool branch line, April 1963 (Keith Holt).* Opposite page: *Devonport Park.*

IN MEMORY OF
ADMIRAL
SIR CHARLES NAPIER, K.C.B.
BORN 1787
DIED 1860
ERECTED 1863
BY THE
SEAMEN, MARINE-ARTILLERY
AND MARINES OF

Beyond the heart of old Devonport life in this part of town went on pretty much as normal. Bomb sites were gradually in filled, generally with properties that were similarly proportioned to those that they were replacing, and railway lines were closed.

The old southern route into Plymouth through Ford (Devon) Station was closed in September 1964 as all rail traffic was transferred to the line that ran via Keyham and Ford Halt, thus rendering the great Ford Viaduct, redundant. The impressive seven-arched construction was busy right up until the end, with Ford Station accommodating no less that thirteen commuter trains a day into Plymouth (Ford Halt, incidentally, at the other end of Station Road, had ceased operating as a halt during the war, in October 1941 after enemy bombs had damaged the platforms).

Two months after Ford Station closed the local cinema, the Ford Palladium, at the bottom of Ford Hill, also closed. 'Economic circumstances' were cited, and 15 November 1964 was a sad day for the local community. There had been an entertainment emporium - the Theatre Metropole - on the site since the early 1890s: it had become the Ford Palladium in 1912 after a three-month refurbishment.

Television had seen off many cinemas up and down the country. It also helped remove the crowds that made cycle speedway viable, although so too did building on the bomb sites.

Curiously enough, traffic up and down St Levan Road increased dramatically after the closure of the Albert Gate in 1966 and St Levan Gate became the principal dockyard entrance.

Top left: *Looking down Albert Road.* Bottom left: *Looking down Haddington Road.* Above: *Ford Station.*

View from the Blockhouse at Stoke, looking north across the St Levan Road viaducts.

The increase in road traffic across the Fifties and Sixties put added pressure on the various approaches into and out of the City, and, in a westerly direction, throughout the Fifties that meant either the Torpoint or Saltash Ferry.

At Torpoint there had been a gradual extension of services. By the end of the Sixties, the quarter-hourly crossing was starting at 6.45am, rather than 7.45am (although it was still the later time at the weekend) and running through to 9.45pm after which time the service went half-hourly. But even there there was improvement, as this facility now kept going to 1.15am rather than midnight. Thereafter the service was hourly. The price was always the same though, sixpence for motorcycles, two bob (10p) for a car and nine shillings for a coach or heavy goods vehicle. Interestingly enough, that represented a 10% reduction on the previous decade, while the tariff for cars was up by 33% - pedestrians happily were now spared the tuppenny levy.

The situation at Saltash had been similar, but after the last ferry from St Budeaux at 11.15pm there had been no further ferry until 5am, all of which meant a long night in the car, or an inconvenient detour for those heading into or out of the city in the middle of the night after some engagement or other.

Dennis Putt, vocalist with Ted Coleman's dance band, recalls many a long hour spent in drummer Frank Barnes' Standard Vanguard, waiting for the five o'clock ferry after a late-night gig in Cornwall.

However, all that was about to come to an end, as, after years of campaigning and planning, proposals to build a road bridge between Saltash Passage and Saltash were about to be realised, but not before Brunel's Royal Albert Railway bridge had celebrated its centenary in May 1959. As part of the party the bridge was illuminated in spectacular fashion, providing a wonderful photo opportunity for all those with cameras capable of taking good night-time images.

A few weeks after the centenary had been celebrated, the Cleveland Bridge and Engineering Company from Darlington were awarded the contract to erect a road bridge alongside Brunel's masterpiece.

Left: *Two views of the Torpoint Ferry.*

The days of the Saltash Ferry were now well and truly numbered. One or two tears were shed, but for the most part it was time to celebrate again. The Saltash Ferry had only been able, subject to cubic capacity and laden weight, to transport little more than fifty cars an hour in either direction (Torpoint with two could handle twice that) and consequently there were regularly queues and congestion on both sides of the river.

The bridge was one of a number of solutions proposed by the Consultants brought in by a joint committee of Plymouth City Council and Cornwall County Council - one of the other alternatives suggested by the Engineering firm of Mott, Hay and Anderson was a tunnel from Weston Mill to Looking Glass Point, Cornwall. The bridge won out as the cheaper option.

Thus it was, on 23 October 1961, that five rockets were fired across an inky-black sky above the River Tamar, to mark the last ever trip of the Saltash Ferry. That night, at the bar of the Ferry House Inn at Riverside, near the eastern landing point, the Irish landlord, Mike Goulding was quoted as saying that the Inn would keep its name: *'It will remind people of the good old days.'*

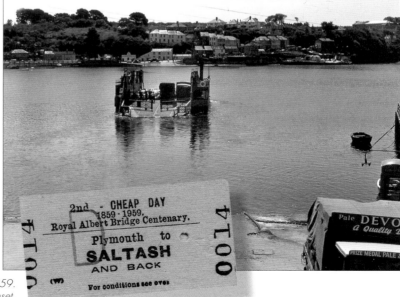

Top left: *Brunel's Royal Albert Bridge is lit to celebrate its centenary in 1959.*
Right: *Two views of the Saltash Ferry with ticket inset.*

ROADS AND BRIDGES

Work on the Tamar Road bridge began on 7 July 1959, and was divided into four main phases, all of which had to be carried out consecutively: firstly, the construction of the foundations and the anchorages, secondly, the construction of the main and side towers, thirdly, the construction of the main suspension cables and finally the erection of the suspended structure - the bit that carried the road.

Before any work was carried out tests were done at around 40 feet below OD (ordnance datum or mean sea level, which in this country is based on figures taken at Newlyn nearly 100 years ago). This was to make sure the rock base would support the great, hollow-legged towers that were going to support the structure.

Each two-legged tower was to be 240 ft high, with the tapering legs being 50ft apart. Work on the towers was dogged by excessive rainfall, nevertheless the towers grew steadily. The rain

also impacted on the four tunnels being dug behind the side towers to anchor each end of the massive cables that were in preparation. Flooding slowed progress, as did the hardness of the rock being excavated.

The anchor tubes and frames themselves were made up of a large number of seamless steel tubes, each one almost 20 yards long, carefully splayed from the entrance to the rear of each tunnel and held in place by steelwork. Once this operation had been completed the tunnels were filled with concrete. High tensile steel rods were then slipped into each tube and the loose ends fitted with nuts ready to receive the massive cables, each made up of 31 pre-stressed ropes. It was essential that all the metal work was pre-stressed so as to eliminate variations caused by loading and temperature, and to make sure, obviously enough, that everything sagged in the same way.

Left: *Aerial view showing that work on the footings has already started.* Above: *Work on the towers begins and note the anticipated completion date - 4 August 1961.* Opposite page: Right: *Men line up as the tower is ready.* Left: *Ready to take the cables.*

Stress was an important consideration, affecting both the loading of the metal work, and the engineers doing their calculations ... and the men who had to put everything physically in place.

'There were three main gangs working the job: one based on the Plymouth side, one at Saltash and the "over the water gang" which was us,' recalled George Woolaway, who was working on the bridge with his brother, Dave. Both men were in their twenties and there was no doubt that the work wasn't for the fainthearted.

'No hard hat and a pair of slip-on shoes - that's me with my legs dangling over the edge - I feel sick when I look at these pictures now,' said George some 50 years later. George had joined the job in 1960, Dave had been there since the beginning: *'There was about 30 of us there, carpenters and labourers ... Ted Lawton was the foreman. That was before the steel started coming on site. When that happened we were transferred to sorting out all the shuttering for all the concrete to go over the steels and make the towers. We spent a year or so on that. Then the steel erectors did the cables and we had to baton out the catwalks so that it wasn't too slippery when the chain links were wet. We went all the way across on both sides, there were three of us on each side: I was on the north side. Then we had to go along the cables putting clamps on them in readiness*

Left, top and bottom: *With the suspension cables in place the first of the framework sections for the road is lifted into place.* Right: *Looking up - but it's a long way down - note the boat!*

for the binding machines to come along and fix the cables.'

Dave was once tipped out of his perch 200 feet up above the Tamar, when a stand-in crane operator misread his hand signals and eased him down rather than up. The big 'bucket' he was in hit a fitting and Dave was tipped out. Fortunately he managed to grab hold of a cable and slide down it more than 100 feet before safely arriving at the bottom, with some rather nasty burns on his hands.

Tragically there were a couple of other more serious incidents:

'One guy fell off on the Plymouth side and one in the middle, who was working on the other side of the bridge from me when the swinging metal cage – canary perch – he was standing on just swung out from the side and he was tipped out trying to regain his footing on a board that had slipped out. The boards we were working on were just resting in place and were only six inches wide ... I can still see him falling through the air.'

Neither of the two men survived and the tally of those lost on the project rose even higher when a group of workmen, not wanting to wait for the old Saltash ferry to bring them back to Plymouth, used a boat the bridge people had hired, but sadly there were too many in it and the boat capsized.

Six men were lost.

Left: *The steel erectors enjoy a pint in the Victory Inn: Back row; left to right, Dave and George Woolaway, Tommy Williams, Johnny May, Dick Levers, Johnny Kiley and A.N. Other. Middle; Freddy 'the firefly' Vickery, ? Price, Stan Knox, Tommy Vauxhall a hard man and the man in charge, Tommy Veitch, Sid Ellis and the Landlord of the Victory. Front; one of the pub locals, Brown, Arthur Fox, Tom, Geordie, Gerry Price and Frankie Webber.* Right: *The above the water gang; Dick Levers, Arthur Fox, Roger Ellis, 'Geordie', Tommy Williams and George Woolaway.*

By March 1961 the structure was ready for the erection of the main steelwork most of which had been brought down from Darlington by train.

In their souvenir book on the bridge, construction engineers Cleveland gratefully acknowledged *'the valuable assistance given to this matter by the British Transport Commission who laid on five special trains to carry "out of gauge" loads to storage areas which they had prepared for the steelwork.'*

'The steel would come as big pieces from Friary Goods Yard and we'd make up sections that would be hoisted into position by crane,' said Dave Woolaway.

Footwalks and balustrades were erected, the road surface was asphalted and by 23 October 1961 the bridge was ready to take traffic. However although open for business from that date onwards, the structure was not yet fully finished and the official opening was not until 26 April 1962. Queen Elizabeth, the Queen Mother, the wife of the great-grandson of Prince Albert, in whose honour the neighbouring bridge had been named, officiated - she was accompanied by the joint chairmen of the Bridge Committee, Sir John Carew Pole and Sir Clifford Tozer.

Left: The bridge nears completion. Above: Steelwork at Friary. Opposite page, top left: The bridge is serviceable but not complete. Bottom left: Queen Elizabeth the Queen Mother with Sir John Carew Pole and Sir Clifford Tozer. Right: Opening day scenes.

Over the years various people have claimed to have been first over the bridge and the honour probably went to one of the workmen, however tobacconist Thomas Ockleshaw stayed up all night to be first across on opening day and Joe Pengelly, of another tobacconist family, was second: *'My grandfather, Dan Brown, had been present at the opening of Brunel's railway bridge in 1859 and as a very old man he gave me a first-hand account of the event, which had been attended by the largest crowds ever seen in Plymouth. My crossing on foot was memorable because, as the barriers were raised the heavens emptied and I was soaked to the skin. My shoes were so full of water by the driving rain that they were never again wearable.'* But even they weren't the first; *'on the evening before the bridge opened to traffic rumours began to circulate that pedestrians were being allowed to walk across the bridge, which is what my family duly did,'* says Michael Greenwood. *'It resulted in a unique journey, as we walked from Devon into Cornwall and returned on the penultimate Saltash steam chain ferry from Cornwall to Devon.'*

For the motorist however, the new toll was twice that of the old ferry. Three shillings (15p), as opposed to 1/6d, but most were happy to pay and avoid the delays they had known before.

Top left: Heavy plant crossing - a steamroller crosses the new bridge. Bottom: Open day for the Tamar Road Bridge, 24 October 1961. Above: Pemros Road in springtime

Pemros Road is the main approach route through town, emerging onto the new picture-postcard view of the two Tamar crossings.

Just as the access into Plymouth was being improved on the western front, so there were significant improvements being made to the eastern approaches.

There had been a bridge across the lower reaches of the Plym decades before Brunel had been commissioned to produce a crossing of the Tamar, although curiously enough, Brunel's father, Marc, an exiled French engineer, had been asked, even earlier, by some Saltash merchants if he could devise a way of bridging the Tamar and had declared that it couldn't be done.

In fairness the technology at the time wasn't quite there, and the Plym was an easier proposition.

Thus it was that on 14 July 1827 her Royal Highness, the Duchess of Clarence (later Queen Adelaide – the wife of William IV) officially opened the marvellous new Iron Bridge over the Plym at Laira. Designed by James Meadows Rendel, a young engineer, who had also drawn up plans for a suspension bridge over the Tamar, the total cost of the scheme was £10,000. The most extensive use of iron in the area at the time, the bridge attracted interest from far and wide and it is a further credit to the engineer that the bridge stood for over 130 years before it was eventually decided that the strains and stresses caused by the greatly increased traffic flow over the bridge were simply too much for the ageing structure. In 1957 the City Engineer was instructed to design a new bridge and two years later work began.

The new bridge was opened by Lord Chesham, Parliamentary Secretary to the Minister of Transport, on 1 June 1961, just two months after the opening of the Tamar Road Bridge.

Top left: *1959, work begins on the new Laira Road Bridge.* Middle: *The structure starts to take shape.* Bottom and above: *June 1961, the new bridge is open.*

Embankment Road in the Sixties - note the Sunblest van and the Nelson's cigarettes advert on the side of the Western National bus.

Laira Road looking across to St Mary the Virgin c.1960.

Having dealt with the two major river crossings, it was inevitable that attention would turn to next to Plymouth's other entry and exit points, the principal of which, at that time, was the Embankment, which, throughout the late Fifties and Sixties served as part of the A38. The construction of the Tamar Road bridge and of the new bridge at Laira had been part of a master plan to remove the main obstacles in the way of making Plymouth a major hub of road transport operations. As railway traffic was being cut back, thanks to Dr Beeching, and as road traffic was responsible for conveying more and more in the way of imports, exports and general internal commerce, so the problem had escalated for the West's biggest city. Ever since the war these issues had needed to be addressed and now that the bridges had been built it was time for a careful revision of the old world, where the A30 was the dominant artery of Devon and Cornwall, in favour of the A38.

Top: Manor Lane, Laira. Right: The Rising Sun at Marsh Mills.

141

The northern entry point into the City was gradually moving further and further to the north, from the top of Old Town Street at the beginning of the nineteenth century, to Mutley Plain at the end of that century, to Manadon in 1939 and beyond Crownhill after the 1967 extension.

The more development that took place beyond Crownhill, notably at Whitleigh, Southway, Derriford, Tamerton and Roborough, the more pressure there was on the northern artery through Crownhill village, Manadon and Mutley. The latter, being later, was better able to deal with the increased traffic flow, but Crownhill could not.

Thus it was in 1967, the year of the boundary extension, which included somewhat controversially, bringing Plympton and Plymstock inside the city boundary, that work began on the new section of the northern route into the city. Crownhill village was to be by-passed altogether and the old Plumer Barracks site was cut through, the surviving buildings themselves not long for this world. The following year the first phase had been finished and the sweeping new dual-carriageway up Manadon Hill had been completed.

Top: *The Golden Hind at Manadon.* Above: *Work commences on the new Crownhill Flyover.*

Top: *The flyover starts to take shape.* Above left: *Civil engineering works at Crownhill.* Above right: *The new-look Manadon Hill..*

Road widening and redevelopment was taking place all over the northern fringes of the city. Before the war there had been two great ancient estates either side of Manadon Hill - Manadon and Widey. The former was acquired by the Admiralty in 1938, while the latter was then owned by a couple of naval gentlemen, Commander William Evelyn Cavendish Davy and Lt Cmdr Geoffrey Dennis St Quintin Marescaux, and there were plans to convert the mansion into a first-class hotel. In the event the Royal Naval Engineering College - HMS Thunderer - was opened on the 100-acre Manadon estate in 1940 and the following year Widey was requisitioned by the City Police.

At first the naval college was housed in temporary buildings, but in 1951 the instructional block and factory were completed and in July 1956 Earl Mountbatten laid the foundation stone of the new accommodation block and wardroom.

Meanwhile on the eastern side of Manadon Hill, the 53-acre Widey estate, after being compulsorily purchased in 1950, was split up and the historic 32-roomed mansion (a refuge of Charles I during the Civil War) was demolished in 1954 to make way for Widey Primary School.

In the event the school wasn't opened until 1963 (and completed the following year), by which time the 'School of the Future' - Widey Technical School had opened (in 1959) further up the site.

Top left: *1968, Widey Lane looking south.* Bottom left: *New road at Crownhill.* Above: *The accommodation block at RNEC Manadon.*

There was yet more development at Whitleigh and Southway.
Until work began on the Whitleigh estate, after the war, the basic layout of the area had altered little since the Domesday Survey. With its manor house and two farms it would doubtless have been recognisable to Robert d'Albermarla, who became its new Norman Lord after the Conquest over 900 years ago.

But all that changed very quickly, with little left to record the old order, save the naming of one of the two new pubs designed to serve the area - the Tiger and the Albermarle.

There were two new pubs too, a little further to the north on the new Southway estate. Southway was planned to be the city's biggest new housing estate, with a total of 2,300 dwellings. By September 1957 the first 300 had been occupied and in 1958 the Junior School was opened, but progress generally was slow and the secondary school wasn't opened until 1962, two years after the date originally planned.

Other facilities however, traditional community-based buildings like pubs, halls, shops, were slow to arrive, and writing in 1966, in an article entitled 'Paradise or Purdah', reviewing the state of Southway, Michael Miller noted that: *'For baby clothes, a choice of knitting wool, curtain material, a birthday present or a pint of beer, people still have to travel off the estate …. It's hardly surprising that there is a lack of community spirit.'*

Above: *Looking south from Whitleigh*. Right, top and bottom: *New shopping village at Southway.*

Having served as the city's main shopping centre for much of the post-blitz period, at least through until the new City Centre started opening up in the mid-Fifties, Mutley Plain started to lose some of it's appeal as the decade wore on and the Sixties arrived.

Most of the bigger stores that had taken up temporary residence along the strip had relocated back to the City Centre, but the Plain remained a thriving and largely self-contained shopping precinct where you could buy just about anything you might want, from fish to furniture, and rattles to radios.

Unlike the massive new housing estates that had been carved up by the big breweries and only allocated a couple of pubs, Mutley Plain was blessed with three - the Hyde Park, Fortescue and the Nottingham, with the Railway not far away, off Greenbank Hill. Throughout the Fifties and Sixties the Fortescue was run by the ebullient Gordon Tregenza, who, in 1954 opened what he claimed was Mutley's first licensed restaurant, which became an instant favourite for the directors of Plymouth Argyle.

The Plain also had two major churches, Mutley Baptist and Mutley Methodist, both of which had thriving youth clubs, and a cinema - the Belgrave.

Opened in 1912, the Belgrave was managed throughout the Fifties and Sixties by the charming and quietly spoken, John Prance who cut a familiar figure welcoming patrons with his pipe in his hand and his trilby on his head. John's father, Guy Prance, had been a pioneering figure on the Plymouth cinema scene.

Top left: *Ford Park looking towards Mutley Plain*. Above left: *Looking north up Mutley Plain, with Mutley Methodist Church*. Above right: *Southern end of Mutley Plain*. Opposite: *Looking sou*

Just as the main arterial road through the ancient town of Plympton St Maurice - Fore Street - had long since been by-passed by the Ridgeway, along the top of Plympton, in the late-eighteenth century, so, by the late-twentieth century, pressure was mounting to provide an alternative route to the Ridgeway itself.

In the event the Ridgeway continued to serve as a section of the A38 throughout the Sixties and it wasn't until the following decade that the Plympton Bypass was opened.

Top: *1968 - the newly built Rees Youth Centre at Plympton.* Above left: *Fore Street looking east.* Above right: *Fore Street looking west.* Opposite page: *Plympton Ridgeway.*

Plymstock Broadway with Victoria Wine, Dingles, Millbay Laundry, Widgers and Fine Fare.

It was on 1 April 1967 that Plympton and Plymstock had been brought within the boundary of the City of Plymouth. For Plympton, that had once been the dominant community in the area, it was a massive turn around in fortunes: Plymstock, on the other hand, was still growing in status.

Exactly twelve months earlier the infant shopping centre on the site of the old market garden in Plymstock witnessed the opening of Plym House - the latest addition of the Plymouth and South West Devon Co-operative to the Broadway shopping centre.

Bringing various departments together under one roof, the new unit included a grocer's, butcher's, off licence, pharmacy, and greengrocery supermarket on the ground floor, with ladies hairdressing, clothing, household goods, a restaurant, bar and laundry facility on the first floor.

A large queue formed on the opening day, and although the customers were happy, the management soon complained that the trade in the menswear and drapery sections of the clothing department was not enough to justify the amount of space allocated to them. So it was that within two years they were removed and in their place a frozen food department appeared.

The times they were a-changing and among the well known local landmarks that did survive the Sixties was the old mill straddling Billacombe brook at Pomphlett, while tide was also turning for Pomphlett Creek itself.

Above: The new Co-op on the Broadway. Top right: Pomphlett Creek in 1960 with the Sanguity being loaded up with crushed stone. Middle: Pomphlett Mill, demolished in 1969. Bottom: Prince Rock Power Station.

Looking across Millbay Station towards the Duke of Cornwall hotel in 1966, when Millbay was still being used to stable empty carriages - the facility transferred to Laira in 1969.

TRAINS AND BOATS AND PLANES

Enemy bombing on 23 April 1941 had brought about the closure of Millbay Station to passenger traffic - although ironically it had been the goods station that had been hit thus rendering it necessary to commandeer the passenger platforms for goods traffic, thus giving Millbay a life way beyond the end of the war.

Long used for the berthing of empty coaching stock, Millbay handled goods traffic throughout the Sixties and Millbay Signal Box remained in operation until 14 December 1969, although a few goods trains continued to run through to the docks over the next 18 months, a practice that finally ended on the last day of June, 1971.

Above: *Frontal view of Millbay Station.* Right: *The signal box over Union Street railway bridge - Jack Doherty waving from the upstairs window - 1971.*

Left: Train at the quayside, Millbay. Above: Looking across King Street towards North Road West.

Millbay was by no means the only major casualty locally however, as Devonport's largest station at King's Road was closed to passenger traffic in 1964 and then to all traffic by March 1971.

There had been a similar situation at Ocean Quay, although that had long ceased to be a passenger stop. Ford Station, was another Beeching cut, while Plymouth Friary had closed to passengers in 1958, but carried general goods traffic through to 1963 and was still used for freight for some time after that. Indeed a new freight concentration depot was built there in 1966, thus freeing up Millbay for carriage storage, although clearly not for that long.

The modest station at Marsh Mills closed in 1964.

Top: Friary Station c.1961. Above: View from the footbridge at Ford - 15 September 1963.

Meanwhile another Fifties closure was Plympton Station. March 1959 saw the last train stop there. No more the daily services to Newton Abbot (4/3d – 21p), Teignmouth (4/9d – 24p) and Dawlish (5/3d – 26p), as well as many other locations east and west.

The motor car was in the ascendancy and there wasn't thought to be much future for some of these smaller stations and, what's more, stopping at them slowed down services. Branch lines were an even greater problem, under-used and expensive to run. And so it was farewell to Turnchapel, Oreston and Plymstock stations.

Top left: *Plymstock Station 1961.* Bottom left: *Laira Bridge.* Above top: *Turnchapel sign.* Middle: *The last passenger (the Railway Circle Special) train to cross the swing bridge across Hooe Lake before closure of the line, 30 September 1961.* Bottom: Diesel hauled engineer's train.

Plympton Station - the last train to stop here was in March 1959.

The new tower block at North Road Station.

The catalogue of closures around the city did not mean that British Railways were not inclined to invest in their services here. On the contrary: with the opening of their tower block offices at North Road Station, in 1962, Plymouth became the regional head office for Westbury down to Penzance - although thanks to Dr Beeching - who actually opened the new building - the arrangement was to be fairly short-lived.

Having always been something of a temporary affair, however, it did now mean that North Road station, with the closure of Friary, King's Road and Millbay, was restyled 'Plymouth' Station.

'British Railways main passenger station in Plymouth is located at North Road,' we read in a Plymouth Profile publication. 'Now rebuilt on modern lines it is one of the most up-to-date stations in the country. From it the Western Region of British Railways operates a service of through trains to the most important cities and towns. These services enable the business-man to reach his customers with speed and comfort in any part of the country in the most modern type of British Railways rolling stock.

'The famous Cornish Riviera Express leaves Plymouth to Paddington at 12.30pm each day and runs non-stop to Paddington - arriving at 4.54pm (5.25pm on Suns). In the reverse direction the down Cornish Riviera leaves Paddington at 10.30am each morning, running non-stop to Plymouth - arriving at 2.45pm ((3.30pm on Sun). The Royal Duchy express leaves Plymouth at 2.30pm and reaches Paddington at 7.25pm: in the reverse direction it leaves Paddington at 8.30am arriving in Plymouth at 1.22pm. This train does not run on Sundays.'

The review of services continued: 'Many other well patronised express trains provide an excellent service at convenient times throughout the day to Bristol, the Midlands, South Wales, London, the South Coast and the North.'

As far as freight was concerned, 'instead of traffic being put on rail at a number of small stations and conveyed by rail to Plymouth Millbay for transfer to through wagons, it is now collected by lorry in the same areas previously served by the small stations and conveyed by road to Plymouth. The same principal applies in the case of traffic reserved for these points; it is unloaded at Plymouth and delivered to the addresses in the areas previously served by the small stations - thereby providing a more expeditious service.'

The situation created new opportunities for haulage contractors locally and at the end of 1961 Main Road Haulage, a firm based in Chiswick, Middlesex, with a branch in St Austell, opened offices in Millbay.

George White (White's Transport Services - Plymouth, formerly Shippers Unis) was already well established there, while there was also WG Stoneman of Clarendon Place, Drake Carriers Ltd. (formerly the Plymouth Transport Company), who were based in Lower Compton Road and British Road Services (BRS).

Top right: British Rail's top brass visit Plymouth, in 1963. Bottom: Peter Williamson's flat-bed Commer fully laden at Millbay.

For people rather than produce, the bus or coach was still a very popular option for locals and tourists alike, particularly those without access to a car. From the City's new bus station at Bretonside there were a large number of excursions available.

Western National offered a wide selection that included day or half-day trips to Torquay, Dawlish, Newquay, Looe & Polperro and Mevagissey & Carlyon Bay, as well as day trips to Seaton & Sidmouth, Bude, Clovelly & Westward Ho! and Land's End.

Closer to home there were regular bus services to the seaside: 54 to Heybrook Bay; 55 to Bovisand and 57 to Wembury Beach.

During the summer season, between 1pm and 8pm, the No.38 went around Plymouth Hoe and Sea Front every twenty minutes, while the more adventurous could sign up for one or other of the 30-mile tours (2/6d a time): one went around the sea front, City Centre and suburbs, while the other took in Plymstock, Elburton, Plympton, Cornwood, and Lee Moor.

Opposite page and above: Bretonside Bus Station soon after completion. Top right: A Co-op Leyland coach at Bretonside in the late Fifties, later still it was taken on by Webbers at Blisland. Bottom right: Work begins on Charles Street.

Self-drive car hire was another option and at around a charge of pound a day plus mileage, was certainly competitive with the coaches and much more convenient, especially if there were four of you.

Convenience was certainly a buzz word in the Sixties and in the motoring world the latest contrivance to further this notion was the arrival of the self-service filling station. Unknown in the UK prior to the Sixties, it wasn't long before the familiar figure of the forecourt attendant was a thing of the past, here and elsewhere around the country.

Locally the first garage to go self-service was the purpose-built facility above Breton Side - Turnbull's garage off Charles Cross Roundabout.

'The City Engineer hadn't wanted extra traffic going onto the roundabout,' recalled architect Peter Rosevear: *'but we organised aerial photographs and came up with a scheme that argued that that's what roundabouts are all about,*

Left: *Various car-hire companies.* Above: *Plymouth's first self-service petrol station - Turnbulls.*

cars driving onto and off them, and anyway there was sufficient land to set it back sufficiently not to interfere with the traffic.

'Having got that through it then became my job to draw up the general concept. The design was one thing but getting it to work wasn't easy. Fortunately Frank Newby, of the Felix Samuely and Partners, came up with a practical means of creating the structure around the central hub. To put those massive spurs in place meant hiring in the biggest crane that had ever been used in Plymouth at that time. It wasn't an easy site and Paton Watson never revealed that the levels around Charles Church were all over the place.

'Still we got the job done after a few major incidents, problems with the screed and with the contractors putting up the spurs all on one side rather than balancing the weight as they went along.'

The garage was opened on 9 September 1964. Stirling Moss, Formula One racing ace, officiated and was most impressed with what he saw, as were the other local garage proprietors at the time; 'They thought we had built a gin palace of a place, it was warm it was light and it was very practical, the lubricating bay had a big turntable in the middle so the cars could be driven in and shunted onto whatever bay was vacant and then worked on from underneath.'

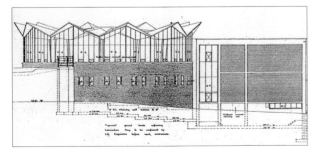

Above: Turnbull's garage between Bretonside and Charles Cross, designed by Peter Rosevear and his father William, who lived next door to George Turnbull and who also designed the pre-war, art deco, car showrooms in Colin Campbell Court (right).

Garages were forever adapting their modus operandi - the days of pulling up on the pavement were well and truly numbered. The Turnbull development represented a major departure from the big tin shed with everything under one roof - but there were still plenty of them around. Follands were a third generation concern on the western side of Laira Bridge.

'Originally the petrol pumps were mounted on the wall, then we had the more modern free-standing pumps right on the roadside. Later the council would try and move us way back off the road again, both to stop the congestion caused by people stopping for petrol and because they wanted to widen the road,' remembered Arthur Folland, grandson of the founder, who, together with his brother David, took the business on in the early-Sixties.

'We had the first automatic car wash in Plymouth,' recalled Arthur. 'Turnbulls later claimed that they had the first one, but we had ours weeks, months, before they did, it's just that, on the advice of the supplier, we didn't start making a fuss about it until it had settled down – there were invariably teething troubles – but that didn't worry the others.

Top: *M Thomas Motors at Prince Rock.* Bottom: *Frank Chapman's garage at the Crabtree end of the Embankment.*

'We also used to do a roaring trade at Christmas,' added Arthur's daughter Tina, who used to help out at times. 'We were the only garage open on Christmas Day and as well as the petrol sales we always had a huge demand for batteries. People would come in, at their wits end, having bought a battery-powered toy or whatever for their children and it had either run out or they had just forgotten to get batteries with it – so they thought we were real saviours!'

Another niche market was that of tyres and, at a time when it was still possible for independent businesses to thrive David Gardener and his business partner Stan May set up the Plymouth Tyre Company in 1963. Striving hard to undercut their competitors and operating on a no profit basis for the first twelve months, the new business quickly won contracts with local bus companies, ambulances and police cars and such was the level of their success that before long they had to take over the upstairs accommodation for storage space, thereby effectively ending the brief two or three years there enjoyed by the Quay Club during its very successful beat group era.

Gardener and Ron West also set up another outpost in St Levan Road - Tyres and Accessories.

Above: Jack Chapman's garage at Crownhill with the roadside petrol pumps which operated with swing hose pipes throughout the Sixties. Top right: T&A – Tyres and Accessories – in St Levan Road, with Linda Horan, Margaret Gardener and a girl called Gloria. Bottom right: David Gardener, far right, with his new Ford Anglia and business partner Stan May, in his sequentially numbered Ford, alongside him. One of their first vehicles is next left with David's brother, Leonard, leaning on the Land Rover. The petrol pumps incidentally dispensed Cleveland Petrol.

One novel way to travel in the late-Fifties and Sixties was by hovercraft, not that it has ever been much of an option locally,. However Plymouth did get a visit from this Winchester class amphibian. Launched in 1967, this particular model (the Saunders-Roe - SR.N6 - GH 2022) was one of a series of what became the most manufactured and successful hovercraft designs that the world had ever seen.

Immortalised by Matchbox and later by Dinky Toys, full size machines were employed by a number of navies around the Mediterranean (Italian, Iranian, Iraqi, Egyptian and Saudi Arabian) as well as a great variety of commercial and civilian operators.

These craft could accommodate 38 passengers (later increased to 58) and GH 2022 was in regular service for the British Hovercraft Corporation (the product of the 1964 amalgamation of Saunders-Roe, Westland and Vickers-Armstrong), ferrying travellers between Ryde and Southsea.

Meanwhile, there were also sighting of an Amphicar in the Barbican in the Sixties, a curious soft-top vehicle capable of doing 68 mph on land and 6.5 knots on the water, oddly enough it was the only amphibious vehicle to be made for private use.

While there was doubtless potential for some sort of hovercraft service locally, it never materialised, but further round from the Barbican, in the 300-acre expanse known as the Cattewater Harbour, there was a very real, non-passenger, cargo trade being carried out along the waterline at Cattedown Wharves, Victoria Wharves and Pomphlett Lake across on the Plymstock side.

Cattedown Wharves were principally engaged in the discharge of all grades of petroleum spirits and there were eleven warehouses available for storage, six of them transit, one of which was fitted with overhead conveying gear for receiving bulk cargoes.

A little further upstream Plymouth's power stations were serviced by tankers of up to 1,200 tons and colliers of twice that capacity landing fuel for the Central Electricity Generating Board. Similar sized vessels could also be accommodated at Victoria Wharves, where the wharfingers typically tackled imports of petroleum, coal, cement, timber, crude tar, fertilizers, gypsum and potatoes. Export items were, in the main, clay, stone, scrap, tar and fertilizers. The wharves were run by Coast Lines Limited, who operated a weekly coasting liner service between Plymouth, London, Dublin, Belfast and Liverpool. Motor vessels Caledonian Coast and Hibernian Coast worked the route.

Opposite page: *A rare hovercraft sighting in the City.* Above: *The Cattewater.*

Top: *Tanker leaving the Cattewater.* Bottom: *British Beacon (launched in Italy 1959) at Victoria Wharves.*

Above: *Roborough Airport.* Opposite page: *RAF Rescue Westland Whirlwind and the Red Arrows at a Roborough Air Show in the Sixties.*

While the sea, traditionally, has always represented a significant and reasonably busy route into and out of Plymouth, the airspace has never really reached anything like its full potential:

'For twenty-five years after the war Plymouth dreamed of a better airport than the grass field at Roborough,' wrote Crispin Gill in his History of Plymouth (1979). 'A Bill was promoted in Parliament to acquire the wartime aerodrome at Harrowbeer, but the Lords rejected that in 1961. The target then became the wartime barrage balloon headquarters at Collaton Cross, but that was killed because it would interfere with the naval gunnery school at Wembury. A third plan for Winston Beacon, west of Saltash, roused Cornish tempers ...'

And still there was no progress.

Roborough's grass field served the City poorly throughout the Sixties. There were charter flights to the Scilly Isles, Channel Islands, the Continent, and even to any aerodrome in the UK, but no real regular services of consequence, although you could book one of the daily 'pleasure flights' and get an aerial view of 'the new City of Plymouth,

the Hoe and other important landmarks.'

Such is not to say that Roborough wasn't busy. The airport was, we were told: 'one of the most active training centres in the whole of England for all forms of flying training.

'It has a comfortable clubhouse for members of the Plymouth Aero Club and a public restaurant with full view of aircraft taking off and landing.'

The City's tourist guide for 1967 described Plymouth Aero Club as 'one of the most active flying clubs in the country.'

It is, they said, 'actively engaged in training candidates for Private Pilot's Licences, Inspector's Ratings, including night flying and radio transmission training.'

At that time the club was operating Tiger Moths and Austers at £5.15s.6d. per hour dual, and £5.5s.6d solo, and Chipmunks at £7.10s.0d an hour dual and £7 per hour solo.

'A Trial Lesson (for 35/- or £1.75) is a worthwhile start for anyone considering learning to fly.'

The children's library with its wonderful mural by local artist Wynne George.

CHILDREN OF THE SIXTIES

As life slowly got back to some semblance of normality after the war, so, in February 1956, the Central Library re-opened. Ever keen to keep abreast of the times, within a few weeks they were offering Gramophone Recitals - opportunities for people to sit down and listen to records - in the Scott Lecture Theatre. With access to recorded music via radio and television limited to whatever could be heard via the Home Service, the Light Programme, the Third Programme and the two television channels - BBC and ITV - such recitals could be quite popular and one or two schools locally also started up their own Gramophone Societies. Although in 1967 the setting up of Radios 1,2,3 & 4 - largely prompted by the success of British Pop music and the Pirate radio station phenomenon (Luxembourg, Caroline, London) - gave the listener a greater range of choice, as did, to a lesser extent, the introduction, in 1964, of BBC2.

But books were still hugely popular and to encourage young people to keep reading in the face of the challenges from the new media the library launched its Good Readers Circle scheme in the summer of 1960.

The following year the Library started offering modern language courses in French, German, Spanish, Italian and Russian and later that same year a microfilm viewer was installed in the Local History Library. Other developments there included the transfer of 10,000 books from the Plymouth Port and Naval Officer's Libraries and the creation of a reserve stack of books in the former St Luke's Chapel at the back of the Central Library.

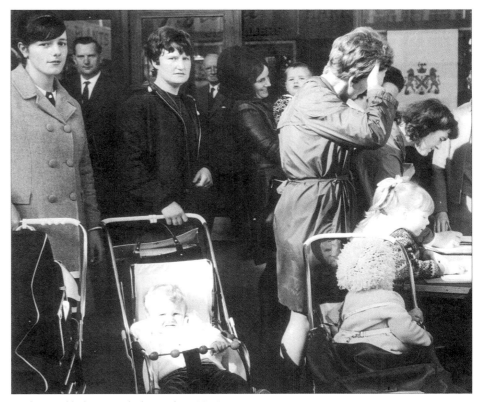

Mothers and babies outside the Market - 1968.

EFFORD SECONDARY SCHOOL, PLYMOUTH

One element that had undoubtedly helped to keep interest in libraries alive had been the raising of the school leaving age. That had first become effective in 1947 and over the next five years the number of school children locally had increased by over 6,500 (around 33%), which meant that when the loss of over 7,000 pupil places during the war was taken into account, Plymouth was well short of school spaces.

Thus the building programme that started at the beginning of the Fifties continued right the way through the decade and into the Sixties. The architecture throughout was unexceptional and made heavy use of glass and concrete.

Despite the national obsession with high-rise housing it was unusual for any school to be built more than two or three stories high. The new school erected in Rockfield Avenue to serve the Southway estate in 1962 was an exception at four storeys.

Opened as Southway Secondary School it was to be Plymouth's first comprehensive school. Others followed and there would have been more but for the resistance put up by the Conservative element on the City Council, who were keen to keep the old grammar schools going.

Left top: *Efford Secondary School.* Bottom left: *Ernesettle School.* Above: *Burleigh School.* Opposite page, top left: *Mount Wise School.* Middle: *Plymstock School c1968.* Bottom: *Southway Secondary School 1962.* Far right top: *Widey Technical Secondary School.* Bottom: *Widey in 1962 with Edgar Harris, headmaster, in the middle and a young Charles Dance immediately behind him to the right.*

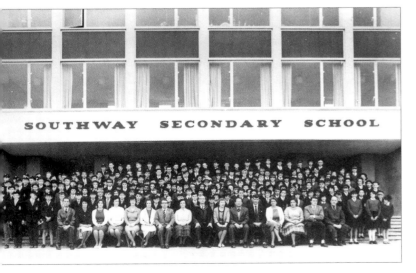

SOUTHWAY SECONDARY SCHOOL

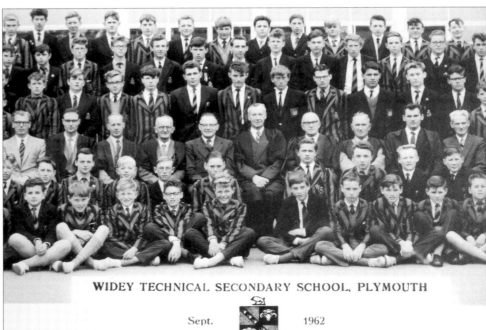

WIDEY TECHNICAL SECONDARY SCHOOL, PLYMOUTH

Sept.   1962

Far left: *Co-op school uniform ad.* Left: *l-r: In the art room at Southway School: Peter Cole, anon, Mr Joycey (the art teacher), Susan Beer, Amanda Spellman, Mike Wills, Valerie Pilgrim, Peter Baker, Steven Kirby and Dave Milford.* Above: *Sixties classroom scene.*

Whatever type of school it was, the learning experience tended to be pretty much the same: a teacher, generally male if it was maths or sciences, would stand up in front of a class and conduct a lesson, with the aid of a stick of white chalk and a blackboard. Sometimes the blackboard would be full of information when pupils arrived at the start of the lesson, other times the teacher would spend a ridiculous amount of time writing notes, questions or equations on the board for the pupils to copy down. Every now and then, by employing a thing called a blackboard duster, the teacher would wipe the board clean - with varying degrees of success - and then apply some more hieroglyphics. The blackboard duster, incidentally (an oblong wooden block backed with a cushioned pad) was often deployed as a missile by teachers aiming to attract the attention of miscreants.

Visual aids were generally limited, although overhead projectors, with words and diagrams written on acetate sheets, were becoming increasingly popular. Here and there you might see an ageing epidiascope dusted off and plugged in, particularly when there were a lot of images to be looked at in the course of a lesson.

All pupils were expected to wear their appropriate school uniform, and it was not uncommon to see secondary school boys wearing shorts - all year round - and caps were standard in most schools. For the girls, skirts were de rigueur - for pupils and for staff - although as the Sixties progressed some pupils tended to hitch up their skirts and see how short they could go before incurring censure. Boaters were popular with the fairer sex in many schools in the summer term.

Ties had a uni-sex status and even underwear was subject to regulations: school knickers - generally black, brown or navy blue depending on the rest of the uniform.

Left: *Co-op school uniform ad.* Top: *In the classroom at Tamar School; George Lacey teaching 5J around 1959/60.* Bottom: *Classroom scene from Stoke Damerel High School for Girls 1965.*

With school uniforms being essentially very uniform there was little room to manoeuvre, however as the decade progressed and fashion on the high street became more and more outlandish so it started to have an impact in the classroom: ties were tied to a variety of lengths, non regulation socks were tried on, and hair, increasingly, became the ultimate means of self-expression.

Boys - and girls - grew their precious locks longer and longer. The side parting was out, the Elvis quiff was forsaken in favour of the Beatle fringe.

The mop-top look was bad news for the barbers, but the industry soon got its own back. As the male population became increasingly self-conscious (and vain) - the standard short back and sides was deemed to be a little too basic.

Young men now wanted their hair to be styled, they wanted their hair to be dressed, and that meant paying the sort of prices that women had been paying for years.

Outside of the classroom, games were still an essential part of every school curriculum. It was true that shorts got shorter and swim wear briefer, but the rules were still the same and there was competition at all age groups - even in primary schools.

Sack races and skipping introduced elements of co-ordination and danger, but bruised knees and grazed elbows were part of growing up for every boy and girl.

As were, increasingly, swimming lessons. The opening of the indoor pool at the Ballard Centre in 1963 created a whole new culture across the City. A trip to Ballard's and the quest for a 25-yards certificate was how thousands of Plymouth schoolchildren (and many more elderly people) were introduced to successful aquatic activities.

Two years later, the opening of the new pool at Central Park improved the City's swimming offer even further and meant that the cold, outdoor facility at Mount Wise was no longer going to be anything like as busy as it had been over the previous 40 years or so, or the venue for swimming galas as it had been for so many local schools.

Top: Hyde Park juniors, with Mr Garland, Gregory Myatt, Chris Wood, Gerald Edmunds, Nigel Fisher, Ian Smith, Peter Colton, Andy Thomas and Mike Cook. Bottom: Robert langman of Burleigh School picks up a trophy at Mount Wise c1962. Left and below: The new Ballard Centre with its indoor pool;

left: Bottom: *Robert langman of Burleigh School picks up a trophy at Mount Wise c1962.* Top right: *Devonport High School for Boys U12 rugby team 1967-8; Back row Pete Reason, Phil Bolt, anon, ry Mills, Paul Russell, Steve Johns, Geoff Birkett, Rob Kessell. Middle row; Robin Jesty, Alan Hocking, Chris Blackler, Peter Williams, Paul Bishop, anon, Hine, Brad McStravick. Front; Chris Bennett, arles Evans, Rob Millman, Steve Oates, Paul Vaggers, Robin Jolly and Mr Trevor Evans.* Bottom left: *Public Central Rounders team: Joan Kelly, Sandra Wright, Sylvia Andrews, Veronica Hill, Janet Brook. nt, Beryl Bullard, Hazel Bartlett, Margaret Lamb, Janet Bettesworth, and Valerie Carbines.* Bottom right: *Sack race at Lipson Vale, early-Sixties.*

1965 Penlee School trip to Innsbruck.

Swimming wasn't the only extra-curricular activity that was becoming more popular in the post-war period. The Fifties and Sixties saw a gradual escalation of the perennially popular school trip.

Day trips to the seaside or moors had been part and parcel of many an education for a long time, and Maker had been a regular destination for local schools for many years. What was different about such trips now was the destination. Increasingly cheap air fairs, combined with a conscious effort to promote peace, and pen-friends, prompted schools to become more ambitious with regard to planning field trips: Germany, France, Spain, Italy, Austria … All these countries and more were suddenly viable venues for a party of school children on an exchange or an educational experience or both.

For many it would be the first time away from their parents, for some it would be their first trip abroad, maybe even their first journey out of the south west. One thing was certain - it was guaranteed to be memorable, as indeed was the whole pen-friend phenomenon.

As well as a means of fostering world-wide friendships, and a greater understanding of other cultures, it was also a fine way to encourage students to try to read and write in a foreign language.

The reward for the labour of translating your everyday existence into another language for a complete stranger (initially) was to wait impatiently for the postman to deliver an envelope with your name on it, written in a strange hand, and with an exotic stamp on the cover - a stamp that did not bear a representation of the Queen's head upon it.

Thereafter lay the prospect of taking the letter off into some corner of the house to see how accomplished your foreign friend had become in the use of your language. The more you laughed at their efforts, the more you realised the fun that they probably had reading your attempts at their language. At the same time marvelling at the subjects that they had chosen to write about and wondering what that choice of subject matter said about your friend - a situation that was equally valid should your pen friend have been from an English-speaking part of the world, Australia, New Zealand, Canada or America.

In the classic American cartoon strip Peanuts, which ran throughout the Fifties and Sixties, Charlie Brown, started to write to his new pen pal with a fountain pen, but after getting ink everywhere he decided to opt for a pencil, and so wrote, thereafter, to his pencil-pal.

Top: 1956 a school break at Maker Camp. Bottom: 1969 Plymouth College CCF at Breckon.

Above: 1966 Peter Lowson and Nick Hale open the batting at Ford Park.

Top and bottom: Boarding house life in the Sixties at Plymouth College

For some pupils in the City, being away from home didn't mean going away from Plymouth, rather it meant living in the city. Plymouth College had been the main boarding school in town for many years. Most of the pupils were day boys, but a substantial number were boarders - parted from their parents for weeks on end, consigned to live a dormitory-style existence with a group of similarly situated peers. For some it was a happy experience, for others it could be more challenging, but generally it hardened them up for later life.

Certainly the all-boys' school thrived throughout the late-Fifties and across the swinging Sixties, with the ever present Martin Meade-King as its headmaster. The school ran an active Combined Cadet Force (CCF) - made up of three sections: Army, Navy and RAF.

Sporting fixtures were keenly contested and any visiting school, particularly the local ones - Devonport High, St Boniface, Sutton, Kelly - took great delight in getting the better of them at any sport. However the school's rugby, cricket, hockey and swimming teams were all quite strong, and generally they gave a good account of themselves.

The other principal independent school in the City was the all-girls establishment in North Road West - St Dunstan's Abbey School - which provided keen competition for the other main girls' schools: Devonport High, Plymouth High, Stoke Damerel and Notre Dame.

1966 Mike Parker and the Plymouth College shooting team. Above right: 1966 PMC

1st XV players Stewart Daniel, Mike Harrington, Mike Griffiths, Tony Burnell, Brian Carder & Chris Brant.

One place that brought all schools together was the Brickfields. Here several schools had their own sports days and here all the local inter school athletic competitions were staged as well as occasional county wide and regional events.

Glorious on a hot sunny day, the Brickfields could also be a cold, bleak and windswept spot, but with schools having little in the way of alternative options, events tended to go ahead whatever the weather.

Such is not to say that the Brickfields was the only venue suitable for sports days, but it was probably the one most geared up for a range of activities. Marsh Mills and Ernesettle also served as sports day locations.

Opposite page: *Chris Brant and Stewart Daniel lead the field in the Plymouth College Sports Day in 1966.* Top left: *A soggy school Sports Day c.1964.* Below: Headmaster CM Meade-King at the prize giving. Above: *Technical Secondary School's Sports Day at Marsh Mills 1960.*

Another facility much used by schoolchildren from across the area was the new City Scout Headquarters at Blindman's Wood. The organisation had been using Blindman's Wood since they'd been forced out of their old home in Buckland Street. Buckland House had been the Plymouth Scouting base since 1929, but with the development of Western Approach, the house and street were doomed, and, in 1957, the City Scouts were offered the Blindman's Wood site for £430. A warden's flat and shop were built in 1960 and then, on Saturday 12 June 1965 the Rt. Hon. the Viscount Amory, the former MP for Tiverton and erstwhile Chancellor of the Exchequer, opened the new hall. It was an enviable HQ, with tree-lined fields ideal for camping, training and games.

Cub and Scout groups from all around the area were represented and among the other dignitaries attending were the Lord Lieutenant of Devonshire, Lord Roborough; the Lord and Lady Mayoress of Plymouth, Alderman and Mrs Percy Pascho; the County Scout Commissioner, Charles Chapman and the City Commissioner, Ernie Cross.

The following year, in June, as part of the Cubs' Golden Jubilee Year, 1,250 Wolf Cubs from 67 Plymouth and South-West Devon Packs assembled at a large gathering in Bickleigh. It was part of a National Pack Meeting to show the lads that they were part of a large body and not just their local pack. It was the largest congregation of cubs in the area in almost 30 years.

This page: *13 June 1965 - the opening of the new Scout hall at Blindman's Wood brings all the local troops together.*

The Girl Guide Movement was also forced to move out of the City Centre. Formed nationally around the same time as the Scouts by Baden Powell with his sister Agnes, Plymouth was slow to set up its own unit. In the end it was Nancy Astor, who, perturbed by the fact that Exeter and other parts of the county already had Guide Unit, kick-started a Plymouth group in 1917.

In the late-Fifties and early-Sixties the Guides were using King Street Methodist as its hub. Semaphore and morse, washing and ironing, were among the key activities, and camps were often accessed via the back of a lorry. It was all quite primitive.

Then, on 22 September 1962, the foundation stone was laid for a brand new HQ in Elm Road, just north and east of Mutley Plain. Mrs D Ledger laid the stone in the presence of the County Commissioner, Betty Bindloss. There followed a major campaign to raise funds, with the local Guides and Brownies all helping with a Buy a Brick initiative.

By 20 May the following year, 1963, the new building was finished and Princess Mary, the Princess Royal, was on hand for the official opening, along with local MP Joan Vickers.

The new facility was styled the Rosamund Stevens Hall in honour of Miss Rosamund Stevens, who, together with her brother, Hubert, had provided much of the funding necessary to get the scheme off the ground. Miss Stevens had joined the Movement before the Plymouth unit had even been formed, way back in 1911.

Top right: *The foundation stone is laid for the new Guide HQ in Elm Road in September 1962.* Bottom right: *Bricks for the new premises are labelled as part of the buy-a-brick initiative for the new HQ* Above: *The facility is opened by Princess Mary in May 1963.*

Keen scouts or cubs generally made reliable lads and ideal paper boy material. Cyril Orton's newsagent's in Victoria Road, St Budeaux, employed several, including Jeffery Greaves (inevitably nicknamed 'Jimmy') and Brian Warne, who were both patrol leaders with the St Boniface Scout Troop.

Cyril, a former insurance agent with the Pru, had a happy band of newspaper boys, each of whom he furnished with a trolley to ease their load, which could be quite heavy – particularly on Sundays.

Ever with an eye for exposure and promotion, Cyril and his staff entered a number of window-display competitions and received a cheque from Pan Books for £7.15s.0d (well over £100 now) in June 1966, for his James Bond window. The display had been promoting Pan's series of ten Bond novels, on the back of the latest Bond film – Thunderball – which had been showing that April at the State Cinema in St Budeaux.

Just as every area had its little troop of paper boys, so every area had its Youth Club. There were dozens dotted around the city: introduced as Boys' Clubs at the end of the nineteenth century they had evolved into Clubs for Young People and were open to boys and girls.

Church halls, basements or out buildings around the country were regularly requisitioned or rented for the purpose. Often equipped with snooker tables, table tennis, and badminton nets, these clubs were run by well-meaning souls who often received little in the way of thanks from their patrons.

1963 Prince Rock Youth Club

Top: 1965: Cyril Orton outside his newsagents in Victoria Road with paper boys; John Drake, Eric Lang, Robert Farquhar, Derek Joliffe, Peter Dunn, Jeffery Greaves, Brian Warne, Keith Burns. Below: April 1966: Cyril Orton's Thunderball window. Inset: October 1965 Ever Ready display.

Many clubs met two or three times a week. Sunday evenings were generally an integral part of the unwritten rules of membership. However, many would feign attendance to please their parents and gain an extra evening out in the company of friends.

Having met and made a gang of mates, youth club members would frequently organise extracurricular outings, although often trips, adventure weekends or barbecues would be arranged on their behalf.

Drake's Island was a favourite destination. Thanks to the sterling efforts of the Old Plymouth Society, most notably Stanley Goodman, the island had been wrested from the control of the Army and handed over to the National Trust and through them to the Drake's Island Council (with Stanley as its Chairman).

Before the island could take regular visitors, over 1,000 tons of rubble, much of it concrete, had to be broken up and carted away. From 1961 onwards, with the support of the National Association of Boys' Clubs, the island would be occupied by up to 100 young people - boys and girls - who would make use of the islands facilities … and help repair and renew the fabric of the casemates and accommodation blocks.

In time dormitories, bathrooms, common-rooms, dining rooms and kitchens had been reinstated and groups of 45 boys, or girls, could be housed in modern accommodation for week-long residential courses. Among the very first intake, over from America, was a young member of the celebrated Kennedy family, at the time when JFK was President.

Members of St Matthias Youth Club soaking up the sun at Tinside c1960

Above: 1960s brochure for Drake's Island Adventure Centre. Right: Stanley Goodman leads a party of dignitaries around the island.

187

Teddy Boys outside the electrical shop next door to the Cappuccino coffee bar in Saltash Street. L-r: Eric (aka Gino – he played for Albion), Dave Bettinson, Colin 'Iskey' James, Dave Knight, Terry, Fred, Bernard Ladrowski and Johnny Hodges.

TALKING ABOUT MY GENERATION

If ever a generation learned to speak for itself it was that which grew up in the Sixties.

The path that those children of the Sixties came to tread, however, had been laid down in the late-Fifties. The break had come through rock and roll, but the door had been opened before that ... by the phenomenal commercial success of coonskin caps, as modelled by Fess Parker portraying the part of the legendary frontiersman, Davy Crockett in the Disney series of the same name.

It was the first truly obvious display of conspicuous spending by young people. Suddenly the world woke up to the fact that for the first time in history here was a young generation that had disposable cash - pocket money: it didn't matter what it was called, what mattered was that here was a very large group of people with some money of their own to spend. Partly it had been down to the raising of the school leaving age, partly to post war prosperity, but whatever had created it, one thing was for sure, a new species had arrived on the planet - the teenager.

The Sinatra-loving bobby-soxers had earlier hinted at the possibilities Stateside, but in Britain it took the advent of skiffle and rock and roll to show young people that this was music that they could make by themselves, for themselves.

The A1 skiffle group at the Astor Institute in 1956 - the Steeljacks and the Checkers were among the other local bands who played at this popular teen venue.

Oddly enough however, while ultimately it would be a slim young Elvis Presley, Buddy Holly, Eddie Cochran-type figure who would make the most impression with the young people, the person who made the biggest initial splash was in his early thirties when he came to the Odeon in New George Street, in early 1957 - Bill Haley.

Together with his Comets, the avuncular figure with his trademark kiss-curl Haley played to two houses on Friday 22 February and while the audience didn't - much to the relief of the owners - rip up the joint, they loved what they saw.

Not everyone was impressed by the visit however: before going on stage, Bill and his band entered the neighbouring Woolworths by the side door and headed straight for the Tea Bar, which was located on the opposite wall.

'This, of course, was in the store before the extension into Cornwall Street, before the Mezzanine Café was built,' recalls John Truscott. 'I was a trainee manager at the time, customers did not seem to recognise the group. The staff did, but did not cause a riot as perhaps would happen today. The elderly Tea Bar supervisor (Miss Evans) did not know what the fuss was about when we told her who her staff had served.'

Musically there was a huge impact in the wake of rock and roll, within a few years it was reckoned that Plymouth had more beat groups than any city outside Liverpool or London.

Top: *Guitar legend Bert Weedon outside Yardley's music shop in Cornwall Street.* Middle: *Mike Tibbs 'I was the first to play electric bass in the city'.* Bottom: *1964 Beat group get together. The Four Just Men (without a drummer), The Pacifics and the Gamblers.*

Top left: *The Fourways 1963.* Top right: *The Chads in Armada Way 1964.* Bottom left: *October 1964 The Four Just Men play St Michael's Church Hall, Devonport.* Right: *Two of the 4 Just Men in 1965.*

The Beatles: Paul McCartney, Ringo Starr, George Harrison and John Lennon at the ABC Plymouth, 13 November 1963.

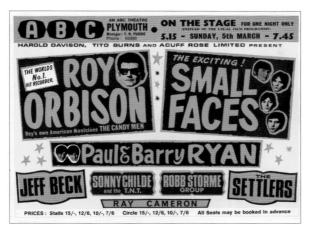

Above left: details of the Rolling Stones date at the 2,500 capacity ABC Cinema. Middle Roy Orbison, Small Faces 1967. Right: The Rustiks meet Dick Rowe and Alan Freeman.

Liverpool, of course, was where the Beatles and the Mersey Sound came from, London was the home of the Rolling Stones and the Tottenham Sound - as the music of the Dave Clark Five was dubbed.

Manchester too had a thriving beat scene, but Plymouth boasted a marvellous musical milieu, although few of the bands were offering anything original, as most were happy to play their own version of the hits of the day.

That didn't make any of the local bands any less popular but it did mean when the big bands came here - those that had had chart success or had been on one or other of the new generation of pop programmes on the television - Six Five Special (1957-8 BBC), Oh Boy! (1958-9 ITV), Juke Box Jury (1959 BBC), Thank Your Lucky Stars (1961-66 ITV), Ready Steady Go! (1963 ITV) or Top of the Pops (1 January 1964 BBC) - there was always a ready audience.

Cliff Richard and the Shadows, the Everly Brothers, Lonnie Donegan, Chuck Berry, Roy Orbison, the Beatles, the Rolling Stones, the Animals, Manfred Mann, Cilla Black, Lulu, Tom Jones and many more besides, all came and played the ABC, most of them doing two shows a day - one starting somewhere between 5pm and 6.30, the other between 7.30 and 8.30pm.

The Beatles came twice. The first time was on Wednesday 13 November 1963: it was at the height of Beatlemania and such was the size of the crowd that they had to be smuggled in and out of the building via a side door, then into a side door of the Athenaeum where they made their way to the Westward TV studios though a connecting tunnel, to record an interview with Stuart Hutchinson, for Westward's own teenage programme Move Over, Dad. The programme was promoted as being *'A gay new show with the accent on the beat of the young.'*

Westward also tried their hand at a local talent show, the short-lived Westward Beat Competition of 1964. The Beatles manager Brian Epstein and the man who turned down the Beatles but later signed the Rolling Stones, Dick Rowe, were judges on the competition.

It was won by Paignton band the Rustiks, whose reward was to appear with the Beatles, in October 1964, when they returned to the ABC. Brian Epstein even signed the band and they released a couple of singles on Decca - What A Memory Can Do which came out that year, and Not The Losing Kind in January the following year - neither was a success.

As well as the Rustiks, Michael Haslam, Sounds Incorporated, Mary Wells, the Remo Four and Tommy Quickly were on the busy line up. Small wonder that the Beatles only had time for a 25 minute set - a set that included their two big singles from earlier in the year: Can't Buy Me Love and A Hard Day's Night. They also played a few other songs from the Hard Day's Night film which had been released that summer., including I'm Happy Just to Dance With You, If I Fell and I Should Have Known Better.

The closest any Plymouth band got to achieving chart success was the hugely popular Betterdays - Plymouth's answer to the Rolling Stones.

They signed to one of the big record companies of the day - Polydor - and released a single: Don't Do That. Sadly it didn't do anything. Music and fashion were then inextricably linked.

'We were Troggs before we were Mods,' recalls ex-mod Frank Moulder. 'We used to meet at the El Sombrero coffee bar, in our Hush Puppies, army-type combat jackets and Levi jeans. We'd listen to a lot of jazz and blues, Thelonius Monk, Coleman Hawkins, Sonny Terry and Brownie McGhee and the MJQ (Modern Jazz Quartet). Later we moved down to the Tarantula and the fashion changed, more mohair suits and Italian-style slip-on shoes. One of our crowd, Robin, worked in Burtons and he'd fit us up for our suits. The detail was always important, length of jacket vents, angle of the pocket flaps, all that sort of thing. The best shop in town then was Jon Saberton's place – all the Mods went there.

'In the evening the Quay Club was the place to go. The Betterdays were THE band locally, but you'd get touring acts too, John Lee Hooker, the Graham Bond Organisation, Zoot Money.'

The Quay Club then, to quote their own publicity material, specialised 'in Rhythm and Blues' and now 'advocates the work, songs and music mainly originating in America, the very country to which the Pilgrims sailed.' The Quay Club was upstairs in a building on Vauxhall Quay overlooking the departure point of the Pilgrims back in 1620.

'Sessions are held five evenings and two afternoons each week and present local and International R&B artists, together with folk singing, poetry reading and other contemporary entertainment features.'

There were around 1,500 club members in 1964 and in 1965 that number grew to 2,000, but just as they were expanding, so was the tyre business below, and the Quay Club was forced out. It relocated to the Forum Cinema at Devonport, where Quay Club membership cards were overstamped with 'The Key', an intentional pun on the old name. 'It got bigger, but our crowd didn't enjoy it as much,' says Frank, looking back on it all, as musical tastes had by then embraced the burgeoning Motown scene.

Top: *The Provokers l-r; Mike Antonucci, Bob and Jeff Biddle, Derek Fletcher and Jean Dignand.*
Bottom: *The Betterdays - Bob Pitcher, Frank Tyler, Mike Hayne, Mike Weston and Richard Brozcek.*
Inset: *The Polydor single - Don't Do That.*

Plymouth mods - an art college study from the mid-sixties with, amongst others, Geoff Westlake, Ted Chapple, David May, Hatti Hayne and Judi Spiers.

'On Saturday nights, mainly in the summer, we used to meet up outside the Post Office at St Andrew's Cross - up to 100 mods - girls and boys. The scooter mods would show off by driving around St Andrew's Roundabout or line up their machines outside the Post Office.

'We used to get suits made up at Burtons for £9. Rob Partridge and I would buy fabric from old tailors to get them made up and then swap them so it looked like we had big wardrobes. Rob had one of the first blue mohair suits in the city: four-button narrow-lapel, 12inch side vents and flat fronted, seventeen-inch trouser bottoms and black slip-on shoes. Usually worn with a white shirt and narrow black knitted or polka dot tie.

'We used to drive to the 400 club in Torquay on Saturday nights when nothing much seemed to be happening in Plymouth. We would wear Levis and sports or T-shirts for the drive and change into our suits, shirts and ties in the gents on the seafront. It was very important that our clothes looked fresh and sharp as we went into the 400 - first impressions for all those London girls that came down on holiday' (David May).

195

February 9th at 7.30 p.m.

**THE
CLOCKWORK
ORANGE**

Nº 116

4|-

Right of Admission Reserved

The Key Club only lasted a year or so at the Forum, the 'scene' swiftly transferring to the Exmouth Road Social Club, where, after a brief spell as the Purple Fez, Peter Van Dike started promoting the latest acts on the progressive pop/rock circuit.

In a very short space of time, music had moved on: Elvis Presley (who never visited these shores, hence partly the success of Cliff Richard) had introduced 'black' music to a white audience and become the King of Rock'n'Roll on the way; the Beatles had then redefined the genre and taken control of the writing and production of music, and through their success had been given the freedom by their record company to 'do their own thing'.

As a consequence through embracing different styles and experimenting with different substances, the Beatles had taken popular music into a whole new realm, one where young artists weren't dependent on Tin Pan Alley songsmiths to provide them with material, but were keen to try new things - to progress the pop process.

Before the Sixties were out, Pink Floyd, the Moody Blues, Jethro Tull, King Crimson, Family, Deep Purple, Free, Yes, Mott the Hoople and many many more had all performed in the cult Van Dike club in Exmouth Road. Meanwhile many of more commercial bands had been booked into the Guildhall, often with local support acts.

Top left and right: *Plymouth goes psychedelic with the Clockwork Orange in 1967.* Left: *The Chimera.*

THE BEATLES | PLYMOUTH HOE 1967

Top: *Pop posters from the Guildhall in 1969. Top right: Frozen Tear l-r: Leeson Burt, Tony Way, John Morgan and Paul Riley. Inset: Their debut single - The Hunter. Right: Commune with Mike Behennah, John Lang, and Pete Isbel on the Hoe Promenade c1969. Above: The Beatles on the Hoe during their Westcountry outing filming Magical Mystery Tour in September 1967.*

197

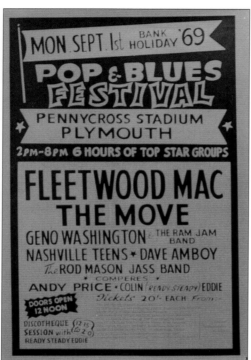

Undoubtedly the biggest show of the Sixties locally, though, was staged at Pennycross Stadium, on Whit Monday, 1969, when local impresarios Harry Greenslade, Bob Jones and Pete Holder put together Plymouth's first big open-air pop festival.

Inspired by the Isle of Wight event held the previous August, with Jefferson Airplane, Arthur Brown, the Move and Tyrannosaurus Rex, the promoters booked one of the biggest names of the day - Fleetwood Mac, who together with the Herd topped the bill that was completed with the Spirit of John Morgan and a number of local acts, including the popular jazz combo led by Rod Mason.

It was estimated that something like 10,000 young people turned out for the gig, about 2,000 of whom managed to sneak in for free (a common situation at any event at Pennycross). The whole show was set inside a giant marquee and was a huge success. Unlike the follow-up staged by Johnny Weight later that same year. Unadvisedly he booked the same headline act, the festival flopped and it was a while before anyone attempted anything similar in the city.

Top left and middle: *Posters from Plymouth's two open air festivals in 1969.* Right top: *The May marquee.* Middle: *Inside the marquee.* Bottom: *Winner of the Look In boutique competition.*

1962 aerial view of Peverell, with Pound's House in the foreground and Pennycross Stadium at the top.

Above: *Cynthia Sherry outside the El Sombrero and* right: *inside with Mervyn Reis-Smith.*

SOCIAL LIFE

One of the defining elements of the late-Fifties, early-Sixties for a certain generation was the coffee bar: Plymouth had several, foremost among them the Tarantula, the Hideaway and the El Sombrero.

The El Som was the first. It was towards the end of 1956 that Danny Sherry, a young sales rep from Nottingham, had first noted that Plymouth, where his brother-in-law who worked for the Admiralty was based, did not have a coffee bar like the one he knew at home. Danny suggested to his family that it would be a great idea to set one up here. His mother, Hilda, his girlfriend, Jean, his other sister, Cynthia, and her boyfriend, Jack Palmer, a design engineer, agreed.

In October 1956, Danny gave up his job and came back to Plymouth. The centre of the City at that time was being completely re-built after the Second World War and many retailers on Royal Parade were still trading in Nissen huts.

'Danny set about finding a suitable premises and a run-down building in Old Town Street was chosen. I gave up my job and at the beginning of December my mother and I travelled down to Plymouth, where we stayed with my sister Pat,' recalled Cynthia.

'Danny and I had never done any DIY before and so it was quite an experience, scraping the ceiling and walls, painting, hanging wallpaper, constructing the bar and making simple 1950s furniture. We worked seven days a week from early morning to late at night, then, exhausted, we would go across to the Bedford Arms half an hour before closing time to have a refreshing drink with Tom and Ivy Elliott, who ran the pub. They gave us every encouragement.

'The name El Sombrero was thought up by my boyfriend Jack, so the inside of the coffee bar was decorated with contemporary wallpapers. Sombreros with red scarves and raffia-covered chianti bottles were hung on the walls. Later on, customers kindly donated ships' pennants which were displayed on the bamboo partition at the side of the bar.

'On 5 February, the El Sombrero was opened by Ethel Revnell, who was appearing in pantomime at the Palace Theatre. From that moment on, it was a huge success. Jean gave up her job in Nottingham to come and work in the coffee bar. Jack also gave up his job and started working in Plymouth, helping out at the El Sombrero at weekends.

'After a brief period of time, Danny started employing staff. My mother ran the kitchen, I ran the bar in the daytime and Danny ran it at night. There were only two choices of coffee, espresso or cappuccino, or as the customers called it "frothy coffee". The price of one shilling for a small cup (five pence today) was considered expensive at the time.

'One memory I have of that time is of parents coming to see if the El Sombrero was a suitable place for their teenage schoolchildren to meet socially after school. They agreed that it was.'

Danny Sherry with his sister Cynthia and Jack Palmer.

Left: An unusual juke box hit at the Hideaway Murray-Walker's commentary on the Isle of Man TT. Above: Outside the Hideaway Cafe c.1961.

The El Som proved to be a very popular haunt, the young, budding actor Charles Dance was a regular, as was Peter Vosper, of Vospers Motors, Mike Brown, who would later open up Mr Bee's Fun Factory, David May, Clive Robertson, and Peter Organ.

'I met my wife there,' says Peter, who recorded in his diary after their first encounter: 'Met Jean, she seems nice.'

'Then, a day or so later: "Saw Jean again in the El Sombrero".'

'For about two weeks I had various references to Jean. It was most odd, because my wife is actually called Joan. So I showed her my diary and she said "Yes that's right you called me Jean for our first few dates, but I didn't like to say anything!".'

Although there was inevitably same overlap, the different coffee bars tended to attract their own clientele. 'No Brylcreem or stilettos to be found in our company' noted Hatti Hayne who married Mike Hayne, singer with the Betterdays.

Hatti, a regular at the El Som, also recalled the Tarantula: 'It had a cellar club where the group played under the grille in the pavement; a very miniature version of Liverpool's Cavern Club.'

The Hideaway, meanwhile, was a popular venue for the local 'ton-up' boys - or at least boys with bikes.

'A lot of people referred to us as "Rockers" but really we were just a bunch of young people who liked bikes,' said Daryle Gay, who met his future wife at the Hideaway. 'We'd sit around and spend hours talking about bikes - British bikes: Matchless, Nortons, BSAs, Ariels, Triumphs, Royal Enfields ...

'Every Sunday around 20-30 of us would meet up at the Hideaway - it was tucked in behind the Central Library, at the end of Regent Street, just before you came out onto Tavistock Road. Then we'd head off on a cycle trip to Drumbridges or Totnes or Newton Abbot. We'd form a great long procession, snaking our way along the road in convoy.

'The number thing on our helmets was a trend that started in London. Other towns started following suit. Plymouth was No.7 - Torquay was No.9. We were all bike mad.

'Barbara and David Reynolds ran the place, and it wasn't unusual for people to be there drinking coffee through to two or three o'clock in the morning.

'I remember they had a jukebox there with all the usual pop stuff, but there was also a record that had Murray Walker commentating on Mike Hailwood winning the Isle of Man TT Race.'

Top right: *Inside the Hideaway*. Bottom right: *A cafe on the moor.*

1966 scooter group includes Bob Skelly, Pete Goad, Kev Staples, Pete Deacon, Mike Short. Standing at the back: Tom and Arthur Folland, Pete Van Pragg and Burt Symonds (both sat on the wall).

Motorbikes weren't the only form of two-wheeled motorised transport available to the young generation - there was also the scooter.

'September 1955 saw the forming of the Plymouth & District Lambretta Club,' recalled Len Hocking, 'and the following members were recruited; Fred Avery (Captain), Bill Hutchings (Secretary and Route Planner), Len Hocking (Treasurer), Ray and Pauline Horn, Muriel and Jack Durant, Ray Coombs, Audrey and Neil Duggan, Derek Pearce, John Jewell, Godfrey Hamley, Tom Soper, Joyce Thompson and a few others.

'We enjoyed many runs on Sundays around Devon and Cornwall, social occasions and occasional weekend trips to Bristol and the Isle of Wight, when four or five or us would go off visiting other clubs.

'An annual dinner dance was always held in Stafford William's Magnet Restaurant in Cornwall Street, and many of the King's of Oxford staff attended.'

Meanwhile Alan Wilkinson recalled working as a 15-year-old junior salesman at King's of Oxford in 1959 on £2.10s a week: 'I worked there with Ray Steers until he set up his own shop in Cobourg Street.'

Pike & Co., in Millbay Road was another main outlet for scooters, especially Lambrettas.

As the Sixties progressed, however, four wheels gradually superseded two, in most, but not all cases.

Top left: Ray Steers Scooter Services Sales and Repairs c.1960. Middle: Trade show c.1959. The scooters came in two colour-ways red and white, and blue and white. Right: Show time at Yeo's; Ray Steers, far right and his mate Gerry Tucker (both then from King's of Oxford who had a garage at the top of St Levan Road) help a bevy of beauties at a clothes show at Yeo's circa 1958. Above: Outside the Leigham Hall, West Hoe, where CPO John Jewel; and Tina Tovey, who were Spiritualists, had their wedding blessed – note the garage further up the hill. Len Hocking and June Southay are on the bike in front.

Top left: *Ballroom dancing in the Guildhall c.1960.* Top right: *Ted Coleman's band at the opening of the Drake Cinema.* Above left: *Victor Silvester smiling at Charles and Fances May at a Tecalemit Ball in 1958.* Above right: *Dancing in the Prince Regent.*

More generally though, particularly if you were restricted to shank's pony, just your own two legs, there were a variety of other places for the young and young at heart to enjoy, particularly if they enjoyed dancing.

There was the La Rocka on Mutley Plain, the Rooftop Club and the Park Ballroom above Burtons in Old Town Street, the Top Twenty Club near the top of Royal Parade and, from 1963, the Majestic Ballroom in part of what had been the Gaumont Cinema - rechristened the Odeon, it occupied the other part of the building.

Facing increasing competition from television, cinemas were on the wane. Meanwhile a new phenomenon was sweeping the country by storm - the discotheque. Although music had been available on disc throughout the twentieth century it was only now that the potential for getting people to congregate and dance to discs was starting to be realised.

It was bad news for the dance bands - although several kept working the Plymouth ballroom circuit throughout the Sixties - among them Frankie Fuge, Les Watts and Harry Pook, who was a regular at various venues, especially the Majestic. It was also bad news for the beat groups, as the increased availability of pop music on the radio meant that increasingly audiences wanted to hear the original sounds, only louder than their radios would allow.

Hence the popularity of the amplified record decks.

Bobby Cee (Robert Cattrall) worked at the Majestic, originally as a Ballroom Attendant: *'Freddie Woods, the senior staff supervisor, kitted me out with a pair of black evening trousers, white shirt, stringy green tie, and an outrageous green dinner jacket with black lapels.*

'The pay was 17/6d a shift, 7.30-10.30pm Mondays and Thursdays, 7.30-11.30pm on Wednesdays, including a Supercab taxi home. Tuesdays and Fridays were private functions which could go on until midnight or 1am, for which there would be extra pay and a taxi; on Saturdays there were three shifts: mornings 9.30am-midday (for children aged 5-14 - admission 1/-), afternoons 2pm-4.30pm (admission 2/6d with a bar until 2.30pm) and evenings 7.30-11.45pm). Sundays were given over to Strict Tempo Dancing.'

Bobby hadn't been working there long, when his friend and DJ at the Majestic, Mike Turner, missed a Saturday morning through illness: *'I soon found myself behind a pair of turntables, the ceiling lights flashing in time to the music. There were around 700 kids in the Ballroom - most walking arm in arm around the dance floor - girls of ten years old or more, eyeing boys they hoped to meet in the dark depths behind the dais or stage where they could kiss and cuddle before being apprehended by an attendant.*

'I had heard the DJ's on Radio Luxembourg - Fabulous 208! I could try it! Play an instrumental, Green Onions - say a few words and remember, don't mumble.'

'There was a very strict dress code - boys were turned away for wearing two-tone shoe-laces and girls weren't allowed in wearing trousers. I saw young lads with scissors cutting their hair in the queue because they were told it was too long.'

Another favourite venue was the YMCA where for some time there was a regular stream of the top trad bands of the era, including Monty Sunshine with local boy, and protégé of Frankie Fuge, Rod Mason.

Another popular haunt was Virginia House where another local jazz player cut his teeth - Mike Westbrook. A student at Plymouth Art College, Mike was working at Westward as a set painter when he started forming his own bands in the late-Fifties. In the late-Sixties he released his first few albums on the Deram label, winning international acclaim. So too did John Surman (ex-Devonport High School) a clarinetist/saxophonist who would win many international Downbeat Jazz polls. Often playing with Mike, he was a regular at Ronnie Scott's and made his debut album - John Surman - in 1968.

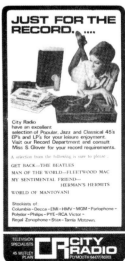

Top right: Bobby Cee (aka Robert Cattrall) Middle: Majestic DJ Mike Turner. Above: Sixties albums by Mike Westbrook and John Surman - always available at Pete Russell's Hot Record Store.

The entrance to the Majestic ballroom was on the corner with Flora Street, to the east of the main entrance to the old Gaumont. In 1962, with the closure of the old Regent in New George Street, the Gaumont was renamed the Odeon, a name that the Regent had carried since 1940. The Rank Organisation had taken control of both the Odeon and Gaumont circuits, and generally when they found they had two cinemas operating near to each other it was the practice to close one - usually the Gaumont. As it happened, it had always been the intention to demolish the old Regent, anyway, as part of the City Centre redevelopment. It's interesting to note that the two venues had opened within weeks of each other in November 1931.

Another cinema to have been opened that decade was the ABC in what had been George Street. Opened in 1938 it survived the war intact. However, sufficient other picture houses had been lost during the war to prompt 20th Century Fox to build a brand new facility on the edge of Derry's Cross Roundabout. It was intended to be the first of a major chain across Europe. In the event it was the only one to be built.

Designed by Leonard Allen and erected by Dudley Coles, the Drake opened on 6 June 1959. Film stars Richard Todd and the 'shapely 20-year-old,' Jackie Collins, were there on opening night (they'd just finished filming Intent to Kill).- South Pacific (following the Plymouth Story) was the first major film to be shown here - it was on screen for a total of eleven months and was seen by thousands of Plymothians..

Above: The Odeon opened as the Regent in November 1930. Top right: The new Odeon, opened as the Gaumont in November 1930.

Left: *ABC in 1963.* Above: *True Grit at the ABC.* Right: *An early shot of the Drake Cinema (showing the 1955 film Daddy Long Legs. Below left and right: the ABC and Drake Cinemas at night.*

Above: *1962 Plaza Cinema showing the cult double bill the Demon Doctor and Varan the Unbelievable. Top right: The old Ford 'Bug House'.*

Opened in 1934 the ABC Plaza at Bretonside was another wartime survivor, however it was sold by the ABC chain in 1964 and it was restyled Studio 7. In this guise the venue soon garnered a reputation for showing one or two of the sort of 'x' rated films that would not readily get shown at some of the other picture palaces in town.

However at least it remained open, unlike the Ford Palladium which closed for good as a cinema at the end of 1964, the proprietor, Cyril Charters, citing 'economic reasons'.

In Union Street both the Palace and the Grand Theatres made it through the Blitz, the latter, however, sustained a certain amount of damage - its dressing rooms were largely destroyed. Converted to a cinema a few years before the war, there were plans, as late as the 1950s, to rebuild it and in 1951 the Council had agreed to protect the Grand until 2001. Sadly the driving force behind the scheme most likely to succeed, Mr EFH Davey, a part-owner, was advised by his doctor to avoid too much anxiety and hard work, so the theatre was sold and in 1963 it was pulled down.

The Palace was also experiencing uncertainty. Closed in 1956, it reopened the following year with a string of slightly risqué shows - like Passionate Youth and Fanny Get Your Fun - but still it struggled and within a year or so of the Drake Cinema opening, it closed again.

In 1961 it was sold (for £15,000) and under the management of George Roseman staged a brief run of fine shows, including appearances by the D'Oyly Carte and Festival Ballet. But then, in 1963 - the year after the Hoe Summer Theatre, and two years after the Athenaeum, had arrived to poach much of its potential audience - the curtain dropped again. This time it didn't close altogether, but, following the lead of the Forum (Devonport's last surviving cinema) it re-emerged as a Bingo Hall and strip joint - the Pussycat Club. The two attractions operating in different parts of the building!

Occasional shows were staged in the main auditorium, there was a notable run of Gang Shows, but little else.

Top left: The doomed Grand Theatre. Top: EMI introduce Bingo to the Palace Theatre. Above: Scene from a Sixties Gang Show at the Palace

Prior to the opening of the Hoe Summer Theatre the City Council had provided tourist and locals alike with the Hoe Summer Marquee - or 'that pole' as it was lovingly described by some.

Hedley Claxton had devised and presented three summer *'Gaytime'* shows there in succession, and in 1962, on the opening night of a fifteen-week run in the new theatre, Hedley was quoted as saying how thrilled he was with the new premises and delighted that Plymouth now had a little theatre that was a credit to the City and the people who ran it.

On the same night, Gordon Peters, the star of the show, was presented with a miniature pole, courtesy of the Corporation, as a memento of the old tent that he and many others had appeared in.

The previous year, incidentally, had seen the opening of the Athenaeum - a replacement for the pre-war building on the same site, with the same name, the new premises was more of a theatre than a library, lecture theatre or museum than it had been of old, but all those elements were incorporated to some extent.

There was also the Arts Centre in Looe Street, the Little Theatre on the Barbican, the Globe in the Royal Marine Barracks at Stonehouse and the Swarthmore on Mutley Plain.

Above: *Inside the Hoe Summer Marquee.* Right: *Western College Players, Roger Hockeday and Angela Rippon in a 1965 production of Jane Eyre.*

Various views of the Hoe Summer Theatre - the City's concrete bins were painted green and cream in the early sixties. Bottom left: Chorus of Peggy Pattison's 1968 Hi Hoe! review.

Whitelegg's fair on the Hoe Promenade in front of the Hoe Cafe.

While the Barbican's Little Theatre was popular with Tamaritans and Am Dram lovers, a bigger crowd puller was the fair, particularly for the newly arrived generation of teenagers.

As Guy Belshaw noted in his account of T Whitelegg & Sons, Cavalcade of Shows: *'Rock'n'roll gave the fair a shot in the arm it badly needed.'* Fairgrounds had been purveying a mixture of *'brass band, waltzes, jazz or whatever took the showman's fancy … in some cases fairground organs were still in use on the dodgems.'*

But now, while *'night clubs and village hops often excluded under-18s, the fairground drew teenagers like a magnet. A magical atmosphere was created by pulsating coloured lights, throbbing generators and the latest chart records at full volume.*

'Youngsters could be entertained by the showman's patter, music and lights without spending a penny. Most, of course, took as many spins on the Waltzer, Ark or Dodgems as finances permitted. And the Ghost Train offered a brief, secluded moment of darkness in close proximity to your latest clinch.

'The fairground at night was a natural meeting place to hear the music of the day at full volume'. … whoever the provider, Whitleleggs, Anderton and Rowland, De Vey.

The circus too was popular, with Chipperfields and Betram Mills

Above: Whitelegg's fair on the Barbican, 1967. Top right: Bertram Mills Circus in Central Park. Bottom right: The Circus parades through town.

being among the regular visitors to Central Park, often after an elaborate promotional procession through town. It was not uncommon to see a fleet of 150 vehicles converge on the City with crocodiles, giraffes and a hippopotamus among the animals being transported in a variety of vehicles, some of which could be up to 100 ft long.

The lure of such circus animals waned a little after 19 April 1962 however, as that was the day that City's Deputy Lord Mayor, Ivor Thompson, opened Plymouth Zoo. The open plan attraction was built in just seven months on Gilbert's Field behind the Barn Park end of Home Park football ground.

George Houghton was the managing director of the new facility but Jimmy Chipperfield was a co-director and part of the rationale of the zoo was that it had a quarantine area for animals being imported into the country.

Entry into the zoo was just 1/6d for adults and a shilling for children and thousands poured in to see the penguins and sea lions, lions and llamas, elephants, hippos, giraffes ... and birds, and reptiles and sundry other creatures.

Another less regular attraction in Central Park, was the Ideal Home Exhibition with exhibitors as diverse as the Royal Navy, soft furnishers and waffle makers.

This page and opposite: Scenes at Plymouth Zoo - note Argyle's Home Park ground in the background of the images on this page.

Keeping everyone abreast of what was going on around the City were Plymouth's four local papers. Writing in 1968, Crispin Gill, the then deputy editor of the *Western Morning News* (based in New George Street), observed that between them the titles present *'the full range of modern taste: the* Western Morning News *serves all the West Country in a restrained style that misses very little and sells over 71,000 copies.'* While its sister paper, the *Western Evening Herald 'has a livelier approach and though its circulation, a little under 70,000, is much more confined to Plymouth it hardly misses a house in the city.*

The Independent, owned for many years by the Astor family until sold to the Daily Mirror group, who use it as a training office for young journalists, is one of the rare Sunday papers in the provinces and sells much of its 44,000 circulation on the strength of its sports coverage. The group also owns the South Devon Times, *the Plympton weekly paper.'*

From 1961 onwards, however, the local print media was facing a new challenge - from television.

The BBC were first off the mark with a ten-minute bulletin entitled South West at Six read by Tom Salmon. Within twelve months this had been extended to a 20-minute feature with Sheila Tracy in the chair. In 1963 the programme had been restyled as Spotlight.

Top: *The City's local daily papers, the Western Morning News and the Western Evening Herald (during the season there was also a Football Herald on a Saturday).* Middle: *Young journalists training for the Daily Mirror: group includes Rob Partridge and Sarah Cullen.* Above left: *Newsvendors at Derry's Clock.* Right: *The 'Morning News' art editor, Ken Price, with his Plymouth photographers - Jack Collins, Les Bailey, Eileen Booker, Mike Cox, Peter Brierly and John Cook. They normally developed and printed their own pictures. District photographers usually sent in plates or film.*

Top left: *Sheila Tracy*. Right: *Control room*. Above: *Hugh Scully*.

Above: *The Westward TV studios at Derry's Cross.* Left: *The early logo.*

 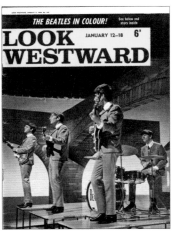   

n 29 April 1961, just seven days after the launch BBC's South West at Six, the local ITV franchise lder, Westward Television, first hit the airwaves. amed by its first chairman, Peter Cadbury, who joyed playing golf at Westward Ho! in North evon, the station espoused its surrounded-by-sea entity by adopting a ship as its motif (specifically ake's *Golden Hind*, from the mid-Sixties onwards). sed in purpose-built premises off Derry's Cross,

Westward didn't have the resources to compete with other ITV franchises when it came to producing programmes that could readily be syndicated, however they did turn out a lot of popular local regional material. They also produced a weekly listings magazine, Look Westward, which ran through the Sixties and featured regular articles by local presenters. The very first edition even had a piece from Westward board member Daphne Du Maurier.

p: *A selection of Sixties covers of the in-house magazine Look Westward.* Middle right: *Smiling for the cameras - Argyle n Leeds United and England international Alan Peacock in October 1967, with Graham Little, Don Arnold and Derek ton watching.* Above left: *Sheila Kennedy and the station's most enduring star – Gus Honeybun (and friend).* Middle: oadcasting the news in 1961. Right: *Filming Westward's popular quiz show Treasure Hunt in the Athenaeum.*

Who wears short shorts? 1966-67 season: Whitleigh Spurs Plymouth and District League II with Vic Bath, Jim Frost, Pete Kelway, Mike Richard and Manager Bill Vickary.

SPORTS REPORT

Plymouth Argyle spent the latter part of the Fifties in Division Three South, having been relegated from Division Two under Jack Rowley in 1956. Over the next few seasons the Argyle board held faith with Rowley after a disappointing first season where they finished seventh from the bottom. However, the inspired signing of Wilf Carter, who made his debut in the first game of the 1957-8 season, saw the club enjoy better fortune. Carter scored 26 goals during that campaign and Argyle won 25 matches, more than any other club in that league, but they missed promotion on goal difference, three goalless draws towards the end of the season hampering their chances. Nevertheless they finished third which assured them Third Division status the following year when the north and south divide was ended and the Fourth Division was created.

Home Park in the Sixties,.

The following season they started on fire, losing only one of their first 20 games, Carter again finished top scorer on 22, with Jimmy Gauld just one behind him. Argyle became the first ever champions of Division Three and were promoted (Gauld left Home Park and would later be imprisoned on charges of game throwing).

Back in the second flight of English football, Argyle had a hard time and, despite another 22 goals from Carter, finished fourth from bottom, level on points with Derby County and Stoke, who both had better goal differences - they all survived the cut.

The 1960-61 season was marked by the introduction of the Football League Cup and remarkably Argyle managed to dispose of Southport, Torquay (after a replay) and Birmingham City (after a replay) before coming up against Aston Villa in the 4th Round. A 3-3 draw at Villa Park was followed by an abandoned goalless draw at Home Park and then a thrilling 5-3 defeat weeks later. Carter again finished top scorer, 28 league and cup goals, including five against Charlton on 27 December - remarkably they won 6-4, the same scoreline that Charlton had beaten Argyle by the previous day!

The following season saw Argyle hit a run of form just before Christmas. After losing 2-1 to Liverpool at Anfield on 9 December - in front of 32,500, they went off on a 14 match run where they only lost one game between then and the beginning of April, winning 11 out of 14 games. Sadly they then ran out of steam and failed to win any of their last six games, losing out on promotion by just eight points.

Nevertheless it had been an exciting season and one that had three big cup highlights, two against West Ham, who they beat in the FA Cup 3-0 at home in front of nearly 27,000 and lost to in the League Cup, 2-3 at Upton Park, and one against Tottenham Hotspur who not only were the FA Cup holders, but had been, the previous season, the first club to do the League and Cup double over the course of the twentieth century. Small wonder that Home Park was packed as 40,000 squeezed themselves into the ground. The pitch was muddy, Argyle played as well as they had all season, and yet Spurs worked their magic. Blanchflower, Mackay, White and Greaves exuded class and Greaves netted twice in their 5-1 victory that saw them on their way to retaining the FA's coveted cup.

The 1962-3 campaign was relatively uneventful for the Greens, Wilf Carter with only 14 goals to his name, top scored for the sixth season in succession as Argyle finished mid-table at the end of Ellis Stuttard's first full season.

Come May 1964 the situation was no better and Argyle only avoided relegation by dint of having a better goal difference than Grimsby. It was time for change.

Above: Argyle v the FA Cup holders Tottenham Hotspur at Home Park in the 4th round of the cup on 27 January 1962.
Right: The biggest crowd for an Argyle reserve match came in December 1961 when Jimmy Greaves made his first appearance back in this country after Bill Nicholson had bought him from Milan for Tottenham Hotspur for a then record British transfer fee of £99,999. The nation's press were here to witness the event and Greaves scored twice in their 4-1 victory. 12,907 turned out to watch the game - some 3,000 more than their highest home gate to date that season.

In 1964 Ron Blindell was removed as club chairman and three new names entered the Home Park boardroom: restaurateur Stafford Williams, builder Douglas Fletcher and the cash-and-carry man Robert Daniel. Keen to emphasise their localness, and equally keen to drive the club forward through the heady days of swinging England, this new board core, together with the then youngest manager in the Football League – Malcolm Allison – determined to revitalise the clubs image. Accordingly they decided to embellish the long-established Pilgrim connection and introduce the Mayflower motif to the club badge. Increasingly mindful of the impact that Continental sides were making to the game they also opted for a new Euro-style shirt with a single hoop around the chest, into which the new crest was placed.

A revised design for the programme was introduced, reflecting these changes and a new era began. The incoming Chairman, Robert Daniel, who like the newly appointed manager was the youngest in the country, organised a photo call to show off a more modern new strip – not at Home Park but on Plymouth Hoe.

'It was chaotic,' recalled Harley Lawer, who was sent down to report on the event for the *Sunday Independent*. 'There were tourists everywhere.'

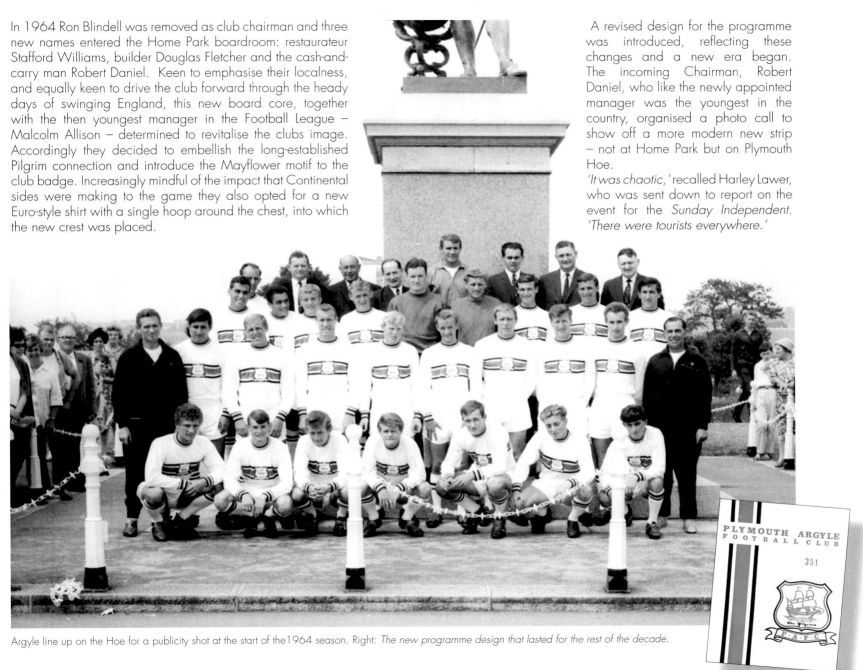

Argyle line up on the Hoe for a publicity shot at the start of the 1964 season. Right: *The new programme design that lasted for the rest of the decade.*

225

The new season started relatively well, the Pilgrims winning 11 of their first 19 games, however after Mike Trebilcock (2) and Frank Lord had given them a 3-2 over Manchester City, in front of nearly 20,000 at Home Park, things went down hill. With no wins from the next nine league games the only solace was to be taken from the fact that by the end of November they had reached the semi-final of the League Cup. A two-leg tie against the Cup holders Leicester City beckoned at the end of January. The first game was away: Trebilcock was on the score sheet again, along with Williams, but the Greens lost 2-3. Grounds for optimism at Home Park proved unfounded when 20,000 witnessed City winning 1-0 and Leicester went on to their second consecutive final - they lost 3-2 to Chelsea across two legs.

The 1965-66 season was similarly undistinguished in league terms, although Mike Trebilcock netted three against Birmingham in the club's 6-1 thrashing of the Midlands club, and newcomer Mike Bickle also bagged a hat trick when Argyle knocked non-league Corby Town out of the FA Cup. Any euphoria was short-lived as they lost their fourth round tie to Huddersfield - the side who'd played them no less than six times two seasons earlier - and knocked them out of both cups.

The end of the season was marked with a new innovation - a player of the year competition: it was won by club captain, Johnny Newman.

Derek Ufton started his second full season in charge with a promising Home Park start: in their first home game of the season they beat Coventry City 4-2 with goals from Norman Piper, Barrie Jones (who two years earlier had been the club's most expensive signing - £45,000 from Swansea) and Mike Bickle (2). Argyle went on to enjoy an eight-game unbeaten run at home. Their away form was abysmal, however, indeed, when they went up to face Millwall on 14 January, they hadn't won a single away game in the league since March the previous year.

Millwall meanwhile, were on an all-time club record of 59 home league matches without defeat and one pools expert, who predicted an away win for Argyle, had an uncomfortable week dealing with offensive phone calls from Millwall fans.

However, after first-half goals from Bickle and Banks, Argyle closed ranks. Peter Shearing pulled off some fine second-half saves and at the final whistle Argyle had inflicted the first league defeat at the Den over Millwall in nearly three years (since 24 April 1964).

Angry Millwall fans stormed onto the pitch, Peter Shearing and Doug Baird were physically assaulted, as was Argyle director Harry Deans, when a fan invaded the director's box. Windows on Argyle's hired coach were broken and a bottle was thrown through the windscreen - damage was estimated to be around £150.

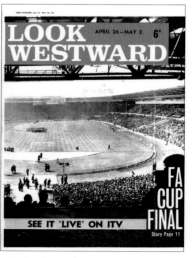

Left: *New Faces at Home Park: Robert Daniel, Doug Fletcher snr. and Malcolm Allison at Home Park – September '64*
Above: *Management and directors show they're keen for a game themselves in 1968: among them Graham Little, George Robertson, Peter Skinnard, Ellis Stuttard, Robert Daniel and Harley Lawer. Right: One of the few occasions, apart from the World Cup, that you could see live football on TV in the Sixties.*

For all the fuss the result failed to mark a turning point for the Pilgrims, they only won one more away game that season, and it was thanks largely to an unbeaten run of six matches (yielding eight points - two for a win) at the end of the season that they avoided the drop.

But if that had been a depressing season overall, what followed made it look positively rosy. The 1967-8 season saw the Greens fail to score in 18 of their 42 league games and either of their League and FA Cup fixtures. Throughout September, October and November fans suffered the agonies of a 12-match run where the only highlights were two 1-1 draws. Desperate to try and raise cash, Derek Ufton sold his best players. The season ended with Billy Bingham in charge and Argyle four points adrift at the bottom of the table.

Back in Division Three, Bingham's boys fared better and, had they maintained their momentum at the start of 1969, when they won six games in succession, may have bounced straight back up again. However, with only two more wins from their remaining 15 games they finished fifth, one point above Torquay United.

Exeter City were then in Division Four, nevertheless the Grecians thwarted Argyle in the League Cup. A goalless draw in the first round encounter at Home Park, was followed by another goalless draw after extra time in the replay at St James' Park. A second replay followed, this time at Plainmoor, and again, after 90 minutes there were no goals, the game eventually being decided by a single Grecian goal in extra time.

Argyle closed their Sixties account by consolidating their Third Division status. For the fourth season in a row Mike Bickle topped the scoring charts for the team with 18 goals, four of them coming in the 6-0 drubbing of local rivals Torquay on Boxing Day.

Torquay had knocked Argyle out of the League Cup at the start of the season. After a 2-2 draw at Home Park, Argyle once again made their way to Plainmoor and for the second season in a row, they went out of the League Cup by the same score at the same ground, but to different sides. Still, Argyle got the better of the Gulls, at home, and away, in the league itself.

Undoubtedly one of the most exciting games at Home Park in the Sixties came in September 1966. England had just won the World Cup and a representative League side brought the Jules Rimet trophy to Plymouth, among them the three West Ham cup heroes: Moore, Peters and Hurst who scored a couple of the 12 goals put past the Irish side. Top: Graham Little welcomes Alf Ramsay to Home Park. Bottom:1966 England XI L-r: Martin Peters, Peter Bonetti, George Cohen, Bobby Moore – with the Jules Rimet trophy, Jack Charlton, Ray Wilson. Front; Terry Paine, George Eastham, Geoff Hurst, John Connelly and Johnny Byrne.

INTERNATIONAL LEAGUE MATCH

Wednesday, 21st September, 1966

HOME PARK - PLYMOUTH

Kick-off 7.30 p.m.   6255

FOOTBALL LEAGUE
versus
IRISH LEAGUE

Souvenir Programme - One Shilling

227

Just up the road at Beacon Park, Albion were, like all the other sides locally, playing friendly rugby. 'It was an amateur game, there was nobody that got paid - you might get the odd player who got a fiver in his boot for a match, but all the players were local,' recalled Sixties' Albion winger Mike Cox.

'You wouldn't get someone from Exeter coming down to play for Albion, although we did get a few players coming up from Cornwall: Roger Harris came up from Penryn - he was very strong, an England reserve on a number of occasions.

'We had a number of players that might have played for England had they been playing for bigger clubs.

'Ron Glaisher, he was Cornwall captain; Nick Southern, he got the better of everyone that came our way; John Gabbitass - he was an Oxford Blue, eventually went off to play for Bristol; Noel Thomas, a Cambridge Blue.

'Essentially, though, it was all very local: the way it seemed to work was that the forwards came from the Dockyard and the three-quarters from Plymouth College or St Boniface, with the occasional player from Devonport High School - like the very talented Nick Vosper.'

Albion would play all sorts of teams, including some of the big sides, like Leicester, or Newport, who would maybe provide Albion with one of their three fixtures over a bank holiday weekend at Christmas or Easter.

Cup games tended to be the only matches where the result really mattered - the RNEC Cup, the Lockie Cup and from 1968-9 when it was re-introduced for the first time since the war - the Devon Cup.

Albion made it to the final in that first season, but lost narrowly to St Luke's College, Exeter.

Other significant sides on the local circuit at the time included Plymouth Argaum, Devonport Services, OPMs, DHSOBs and OPOs.

Meanwhile one of the more noteworthy rugby encounters of the day saw the 1961 County Championship final played out at Home Park.

Top Albion and Bosuns, March 1966: Names not including Bosuns; Peter Jackets (linesman), Roger Harris, Brian Spiller, Paun Venn, Ron Glazsher, Nick Southern, Ian Greep, Ed Southern, Fred Prosser (linesman). Front l-r; Chris Uren, Mike Cox, Gerry Dyer, Mike Richards, Jon Gabitass, Arthur McLean, Clive Cross, Derek Holdsworth. Bottom: Mike Cox snaps Ray Roach scoring for Albion (v Newton Abbot) at Beacon Park in 1965.

RUGBY FOOTBALL UNION

COUNTY CHAMPIONSHIP FINAL

DEVON v CHESHIRE

AT HOME PARK PLYMOUTH

SATURDAY 11th MARCH 1961

OFFICIAL SOUVENIR PROGRAMME ONE SHILL

Albion v Bosun's XV (an invitation side that included a number of internationals), Wednesday 23 March 1966. L-R Doctor Fred Dwyer (referee), James Rodd, Clive Cross, Mike Cox.

PLYMOUTH 'DEVILS' 1952

Opposite page - top left: *Plymouth Devils 1962.* Right: *Stoke Carnival entry c1961.* Bottom: *Speedway action at Pennycross.* This page: Top left: *Marshalls check the bikes.* Right: *1969 team; Colin Sanders, Keith Marks, Graham Hambly (manager), Chris Roynon, Adrian Degan. Front; Dave Whitaker (Capt.), John Hammond, Bob Coles.* Bottom: *Selection of programmes and Matty Mattingly rosette.*

Less than a mile from Albion's home ground, over at Pennycross Stadium (aerial pic), there was a revival of Speedway in 1959, after a lapse of five years.

However the sport spluttered somewhat and after a couple of seasons in the Provincial League there was no more Speedway at Pennycross until another short-lived revival in 1968, when Graham Hambly became the Devils team manager.

Local businessman Fred Osborn, who was also the stadium manager, worked with Devils' legend Pete Lansdale to get the sport up and running again in the City.

On loan from Exeter, Mike Cake was team captain for that first season and finished top of the Division Two Riders' Championship at Hackney. The following year he rode in the First Division.

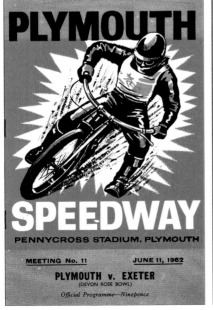

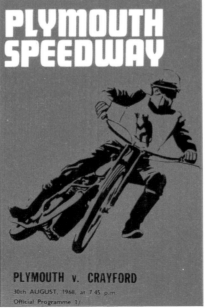

Greyhounds, Go-Karts and Ponies were also raced at Pennycross at various times in the Sixties, but the main spectator sport, particularly between 1962 and 1968 when there was no Speedway, was Stock Car racing.

Pulling reasonable crowds every Friday night, each race would start with the pace car leading the white tops, ahead of the yellow and blue tops, with the most able drivers in their red tops at the back of the grid. Cornish driver Johnny Marquand was a local star, he won the Brisca F2 World Championship in 1965, which entitled him to paint his car roof gold. Another local hero Johnny Sparks was runner up the previous year.

It was a sport anyone could tackle, as former secretary of the Plymouth Stock Car Association, Graham Hambly, explained in 1966.

'First you get your stock car, then a licence (not difficult) and then a vehicle and trailer to get your outfit to Pennycross Stadium, or a friend, attracted by the glamour of it all, with one. And you're in business.

'The cost? It depends how good a mechanic you are, but racing at the Pennycross Stadium is Formula II, which means pre-1948 vehicles under 1200cc and you can pick up that kind of banger for a fiver if you're lucky.

'By the time you've doctored the engine and converted the bodywork you might have spent around £50. You rip out all the upholstery and seats and put in one bucket seat and safety straps. The doors are welded up, all the glass is taken out and one of the windows is enlarged so you can get in - and get out in - a hurry.

'The roof is strengthened so the car can roll over without squashing you inside. Then all you need are lots of pots of paint to decorate the car. And when, with the loudspeakers blaring out the 'March of the Gladiators' you step out onto the track, you can look forward with luck to earning up to about £20 before the night is out. Some drivers have earned up to about £40 at a Plymouth meeting.

'The object of the whole thing, of course, is to get around the track before all the others. In the early days of the sport the emphasis was on spills and somersaulting cars, but has to some extent changed to a reliance on skill and speed - although bish and bash still keeps the crowds on their toes.'

Sadly the crowds dwindled and many of those that turned up had sneaked in under, or over, the fence. Drivers tried to keep the game alive by halving the prize money, but the stars didn't come from up country so often and the sport died away.

Top left: *Greyhounds at Pennycross.* Right: *Pony racing.*
Bottom: *Sports and Production cars.*

STOCK CAR RACING
(Formula II)

EVERY FRIDAY 7.45 P.M.
STOCK CAR
(FORMULA II)
RACING
AND OTHER ATTRACTIONS
Pennycross Stadium, PLYMOUTH

PLYMOUTH STOCK CAR ASSOCIATION

PENNYCROSS STADIUM
PLYMOUTH
FRIDAY, MAY 26th, 7.45
1967 SEASON MEETING No. 5
OFFICIAL PROGRAMME 1/-

Above: l-r; Andy Webb (763), Phil Ugalde (539),
Ron Wood (599), Harry Collins (508), Johnny Sparks
(707), and Johnny Marquand (689). Local hero Johnny
Marquand - the Cornish Wizard - was originally a
Devonport boy, but he bought his garage at Notter
Bridge and adjoining property with the proceeds of his
racing. In 1965 he won the World Championship.
Right: David Crook with his car (604).

7699 AR

For drivers who were a little more mindful of the state of their vehicles there was always the Plymouth Motor Club. In the Sixties they became more and more involved with rallying and in four years their 'Presidential Rally' became the celebrated 'Plymouth Rally'. Engraved on the club's major awards are names that became world famous as rally drivers and navigators including: Ian Appleyard, Pat Moss, Eric Jackson, the Morley Brothers, John Davenport, Colin Walkin and Tiny Lewis. The final special stage of the Rally was via Madeira Road (specially closed for the day), and spectators could stand on the elevated pavement to watch the cars as they sped up towards the finish on the Hoe Promenade.

The 1963 Rally was started from the Guildhall Square on 28 June. Westward TV presenter Roger Shaw flagged off the competitors: he was ably assisted by the station's favourite rabbit - Gus Honeybun.

Later in the year a 'Marina Rally' saw drivers set off at 10pm on 23 November and drive 160 miles. Competitors started out from Stadium Garage, headed for Stag Lodge and then, according to the in-house PMC magazine, *'proceeded to meander all over the place before ending up at Abbots' Island, Lee Mill for much coffee, sandwiches, egg and chips.'*

Hemerdon was used as a regular hill climb venue, but as the decade progressed it became increasingly difficult to stage events. Insurance was one problem, restrictions on using roads less than 12ft wide was another and a number of events were cancelled.

Undaunted, the Club continued, but the golden age of local rallying was over.

Top: *Keith Gorman's 1968 Mini Cooper with a 1964 registration plate.* Middle left: *Start of the the 1963 rally outside the Guildhall.* Right: *A Hillman on the Hoe.* Bottom: *1959 Spotlamp Magazine and the Official Programme for the 1961 Plymouth Rally.* Above right: *Keith Gorman in the navigator's seat.*

Left to Right: *Keith Lovelock (Duke of Cornwall Hotel & PMC), W. H. Gould, Edna Jeffery, unknown (wife of R.A.C. guest), Gloria Ede, June Gould, Guest from R.A.C. (in Formula Ford Lotus), David Williams, Mary Williams, Doug Jeffery (Chairman), Ed Martin, unknown male, Mrs. Martin and an unknown female.*

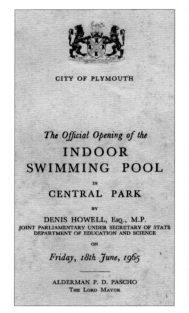

There were of course a range of sports available then in Central Park, as well as the indoor pool that opened in the summer of 1965 there were two public bowling greens, tennis courts, football pitches, cricket pitches and the pitch and putt golf facility running along the side of Alma Road.

The biggest tennis story of the time was generated by the former Plymouth schoolgirl (from Moorfield School) Angela Mortimer, who, in 1961, won the Ladies Singles title at Wimbledon.

Left: Opening programme and pictures of the indoor pool in Central Park, 1965.
Top: Central Park's pitch and putt course. Above: 1969 Reg Watts, Sandra Coe, Janet Brown, Paul Reeder, Richard Oliver at Carhullen Tennis Club

One sport that was entirely new to the City, and indeed to the country, in the Sixties was Ten Pin Bowling. Stamford Hill and Golders Green in London were the first areas to have bowling alleys built, in 1960. Plymouth followed soon after and before long there were 160 alleys all over the country.

No sooner had the game arrived than there were different leagues set up consisting of ten teams of five.

The Premier league played on a Monday evening at the Excel Bowling facility in Mayflower Street.

The top two teams in the centre locally were the Pathfinders and the Mice's.

The League was organized by the centres throughout the country. The league winner and top women's team in Plymouth were the Young Lionesses.

Among the members of Pathfinders men's team was Home Park stalwart George Robertson - George had joined Argyle in the late Forties and played the last of his 382 games for the club away to Newcastle just before Christmas 1963.

Although George carried on playing football (for Falmouth), he became very dedicated to Ten Pin Bowling and held the highest average score in the centre scoring in excess of 170 every game.

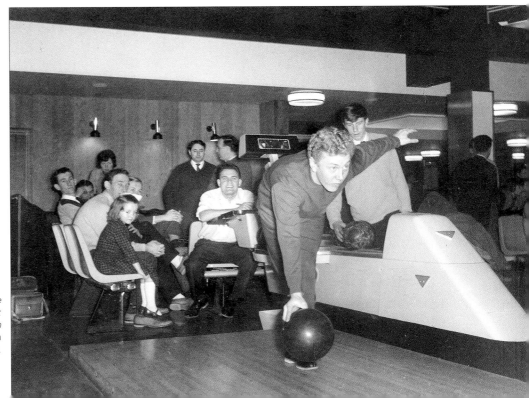

Top left: Pathfinders men's team, left to right: Dave Down, Mike Heywood, Mike Crocker, George Robertson, Chris Maher and reserve, anon. Middle: Lionesses: front row left to right, Anne Radley, Barbara Toms. Second row left to right: Helen Wiseman, Iris Gardiner, Hazel Maher. Right: Mayflower Street exterior Bottom right: The Plymtel team with John Rowley, Ron Hurrell, Chris Rogers, Ian Wanless, John Paynter and, bowling, Keith Dale.

Bowling of the cricketing kind was still being purveyed throughout the summer months at Peverell Park, the home of Plymouth Cricket Club.

The team was captained throughout most of the sixties by Chris Uren, who, when he took over the mantle in 1962 was the youngest player up to that point to have taken on that role. There throughout the rest of the decade and beyond he recalled various highlights:

'I remember in the 1966 season Rothmans decided to sponsor a club cricket competition. There was already the Benson & Hedges Cup for County sides and the Nat West Championship and as soon as it was announced I was determined that our name was going to be on the new trophy.

'It was before the 20/20 era took hold and it was arranged that the competition would start with games of 18 8-ball overs, with a semi-final of 40 6-ball overs. It was our first experience of limited overs cricket and we met Torquay in the final … and we murdered them.'

The following season too proved to be memorable, thanks to one of a number of visits from the International Crusaders.

The Crusaders had an all star international line-up that teamed up England heroes Fred Truman, John Edrich and Colin Milburn and West Indian legends Lance Gibbs, Clive Lloyd and Gary Sobers.

'I remember we had a three-hour committee meeting to discuss whether we should pay the extra £50 that Gary Sobers was asking at the time,' recalled Uren. 'I couldn't believe it, I even offered to pay it myself if necessary.'

As it was Sobers skippered the visitors and walked out the middle of the Peverell Park pitch for the all important toss of the coin.

'As it happened I won the toss but Gary simply announced that they would bat first!

'The game was played in a fine sporting manner however and once he'd scored fifty runs Sobers said that if someone put a good length ball on middle stump he'd contrive to miss it. The next ball was a good one, and going straight for middle and off, but Gary smashed it right over the boundary. The third ball however was bang on middle stump and he deliberately played and missed, he could judge the ball that well!'

In the end the Crusaders scored around 230-odd and Plymouth posted a similar score, but it didn't really matter – the whole event had been largely contrived for its entertainment value and the visitors had been charming … and entertaining.

Above left: Stoke CC: Back row, l-r; AN Other, Doug Kent, Derek Jefferies, A Biddle, John Anderson, John Walker, Ray Banks, John Richman. Front row: Joe Drake, Des Wright, Fred Pitts, Albert Collier, Ed Pearson. Right: Mary Ward and Liz Uren far left, Norman Smith, as Chris Uren and Gary Sobers return from the toss - Janet Stillwell right.

Back row: Roy Periton, Mervyn Kitchen, Keith Baker, John Solanky, Brian Hughes, anon, Peter Robinson, Jack Fingleton, Bert Davey, Peter Vittle. Middle row: Peter Harris, Brian Crawford, Fred Rumsey, Peter Langford, Hilton Ackemann, Len Colwill, Clive Lloyd and Mac Donald. Front row: Lance Gibbs, Graham McKenzie, Chris Uren, Frank Chapman (Lord Mayor), Gary Sobers, Fred Truman, John Edrich, Colin Milburn. On the balcony in front of the window on the far right, your humble scribe wearing his school uniform.

Above left: *Dinghies on Commercial Wharf.* Middle and right: *Plymouth Guides from 1967 and 1968.* Above: *The Mayflower replica in Plymouth Sound, 1957.*

The one sport that possibly defines the City above all others though is sailing. From the earliest days of sailing Plymothians have been taking to the sea, for fishing and trading, long before the activity was pursued purely for pleasure.

Plymouth was indeed a Famous City By the Sea, and who could doubt that it was also the City at the Centre of Things in the West - just two of the strap lines that accompanied yacht themed images on the cover of official sixties' promotional guides for the City.

The waterfront location is the key to its prominence, just as it had been some three and a half centuries earlier when the Mayflower had made its historic crossing of the Atlantic.

In 1957, a replica Mayflower, modelled as near to the original as anyone could guess, had drawn large crowds to the Hoe, many marvelling at the sight of such a craft in a context that had changed remarkably little since 1620.

Ten years later even bigger crowds turned out - estimates ranged from 100,000 to 250,000 - to witness the safe return of the Devon yachtsman, Francis Chichester on the last leg of his epic solo circumnavigation of the world, the first ever one-stop voyage around the globe.

It had been 274 days since the lone yachtsman had left Plymouth Sound and early indications were that Gypsy Moth IV would be back inside the Breakwater by mid afternoon. However mid-afternoon came and went and still there was no sign, much to the disappointment of the waiting crowds, press reporters and impressive flotilla of tall ships, small yachts and little racing dinghies.

In the event it was getting dark by the time Chichester hove into view and so the impact of the fire tender spraying red white and blue water across the surface of the Sound was largely lost on those watching from afar, nevertheless the noisy hooters and cheering spectators gave the great man a welcome to remember.

The Queen had conferred a knighthood on the intrepid sailor (and former aviator) and the Post Office had taken the unusual step of issuing a stamp of Chichester aboard the Gypsy Moth (it was the first time that someone neither royal nor dead had been depicted on a British stamp) and now everyone wanted to see him, but, having found his land legs again, after many months at sea, Sir Francis attended a few public engagements, hosted by the Lord Mayor Frank Chapman, and then set sail again.

Top: *Crowds line the Hoe foreshore for Chichester's return.* Inset: *The commemorative stamp.* Right: *Lord Mayor Frank Chapman welcomes the lone yachtsman.* Above: *Gypsy Moth IV. followed by a large flotilla.*

One of the Navy's great aircraft carriers passes between Drake's Island and the Hoe.

ALL IN A DAY'S WORK

The Sixties generally witnessed a steady decline in the number of servicemen in the City. The Naval presence continued but on a smaller scale than at any point since the war. The Army gradually disappeared, Raglan barracks had eventually been demolished in 1969, after a stay of execution during war. The last infantry battalion would march out of the City at the start of the Seventies, while the only surviving RAF outfit locally, No 19 Group RAF Coastal Command, left in 1968, leaving only a few small units and a few marine craft. The Royal Marines were still in Stonehouse and there were to be commandos at Seaton Barracks and a regiment of Royal Artillery in the Royal Citadel. But overall there was a substantial drop in the number of servicemen seen on the streets and in the pubs and clubs locally.

Top: HMS Salisbury moored off Bull Point. Bottom: A submarine leaves port.

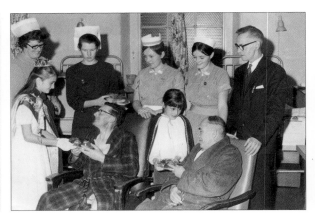

One area where there was an increase in uniformed staff locally though was to be found under the umbrella of the National Health Service.

In 1955 the City Isolation Hospital, Swilly, was renamed the Scott Hospital and in the Sixties it carved out a new role for itself an intensive coronary care unit. The Fifties also saw changes at Beaumont House which became Plymouth Chest Clinic dealing principally with lung cancer, bronchitis and asthma.

In 1963 the Alexandra Nursing Home became part of Plymouth General Hospital and in 1969 two new wards were built at Mount

Gould Hospital. The new development cost £200,000 and was to provide greater care for the elderly. There were also improvements and extensions at Freedom Fields and Greenbank, where a new operating theatre was built in 1958, followed by a new staff canteen five years later.

In addition to the facilities listed above there was the female-only Lockyer Street Hospital, the Royal Naval Hospital at Stonehouse, the Royal Albert (Plymouth General Hospital, Devonport Section from 1963), Devonport, and Gardens and the Royal Eye Infirmary off Mutley Plain.

Top left: *Brigid Stafford with her Morris Minor.* Middle: *Set M nurses outside Freedom Fields.* Right: *SEN Joyce Vance with fellow nurses and patients, 1967.*
Bottom left: *Outside the maternity department of Freedom Fields Hospital.* Right: *Entrance to the administrative block of the Alexandra Nursing Home, 1965.*

Fire Brigade attend an incident at Pearl Assurance House.

From 1943 through to 1965 John Skittery served as Chief Constable to the Plymouth Police force. Strict, but well-liked, Skittery sadly died within a few years of his retirement, in 1968, and a contemporary report in the local press said much not only about the way he himself viewed policing, but how the police generally, in the Plymouth area, conducted their duties during that time:

John Skittery *'adopted a most sensible policy towards the motorist and it has resulted in Plymouth still remaining one of the few places where the motorist is not harried from pillar to post.*

'Motorists invariably get a warning for first offence where minor traffic laws had been breached and he permitted parking at night without lights where the street lighting was adequate.

'He was a tough policeman in many ways but he differed from his colleagues in not regarding the driver as public enemy number one.'

Sympathetic to the motorist, Skittery was also very keen to support sporting endeavours and under his stewardship police cricket, football, rugby, billiards and snooker teams all flourished. Other service sides, other police teams and tours to and from the Metropolitan Force were 'notorious' according to force historian and senior police officer, Ernest Dickaty.

Top: *Officers lined up outside the Council House are inspected by the Lord Mayor Thomes Stanbury. Bottom: 12 May 1967, the final parade of the Plymouth Police.*

Plymouth City Police 1965/66. *Back row from the left: Bill Shepherd, Dave Reardon, Brian Pearce, John Weymouth, Ken Eastwood, Colin Oliver, Terry Harrison, Dave Bowles and manager Maurice Williams. Front row: Johnny Miles, Ron Rickard, Inspector Charlie Burbidge, Chief Constable Gregory, Mervyn Hunt and Bob Scoins.*

So it was that Ronald Gregory, the former Deputy Chief Constable of Blackpool, arrived in the City to take command of the Plymouth force on 1 July 1965.

It was to be a brief reign. Before he'd even had the chance to celebrate a year in post, it was announced that the Plymouth force was to amalgamate with the County Police. Thus, on 1 June 1967, the Plymouth force ceased to operate as an independent body and as the secretary recorded in the last minute of the Watch Committee:

'The Chairman referred to the fact that this meeting was the last meeting of the Plymouth Watch Committee of which the first meeting had been held on the 1 January, 1836.'

And so ended 131 years of the Plymouth Police Force - a sad moment for many, but one that was marked, on 12 May that year, by a major parade of the Force and the Royal Marine band, plus the personnel of all territorial and specialised divisions and the special constabulary.

Curiously enough the merger with Plympton and Plymstock had just taken place and the staff roll had just increased to 530, with the arrival of cadets, police dogs and traffic wardens (who had come in to replace the Local Authority's parking meter attendants).

Top left: *The Lord Mayor TH Stanbury inspects the latest Police vehicles.* Right: *Royal Parade's blue salute 12 May 1967.* Above: *Police road safety demonstration.*

The first of the major post-war factories - Tecalemit, Rank-Bush Murphy and Berketex arrived in Plymouth in the late-Forties, early-Fifties. In 1957 Clarks built their first Plymouth factory at Crownhill and added a second in 1963 making the City their biggest production base employing nearly 1,000 men and women. With financial assistance from central government there was a spurt of factory building at Ernesettle, Southway and Burrington, a lot of it based around light engineering.

Before long, remarkably enough, some 10,000 extra jobs had been created locally since the war, all in all an impressive achievement and although the impetus slowed significantly once the development area status was removed, by 1968 there were no less than 26 new factories in Plymouth — among them Brown and Sharpe, at Ernesettle, Fine Tubes at Estover, and Ranco at Southway, who also had nearly 1,000 employees on their books.

Top: *Adverts for Berketex, Tecalemit, Farleys and promotional shot for Tecalemit c1968. Bottom: Brown & Sharpe factory making machine tools in Ernesettle.*

And so that was a flavour of Plymouth in the Fifties and Sixties. We'll leave you with a few basic statistics of life as it was back then.

In 1968 it was estimated that the population was around 247,680, who between them shared 19,936 acres of land. Over the previous 60 years the mean temperature average had been 51.5F, while the average annual rainfall for the same period was 37.62in.

Everyone then received their electricity from the South Western Electricity Board - the first 65 units per quarter cost 9.75d (less than 4p) and 1.90d (less than 1p) for further units. There was a minimum charge for all consumers of 10/- (50p) regardless of how little electricity was used.

There was just one supplier for gas too - the South Western Gas Board who charged 41.5d (17p) for the first 26 therms and 33.5d (14p) for the next 74 therms ... or you could pay a standing quarterly charge of £2.14.s10d (£2.74) plus 20d (8p) per therm.

And finally ... licensing hours were restricted Monday to Saturday from 10am until 2.30pm at lunchtime and from 6pm until 10.30pm in the evening. Sundays were even more restricted as lunchtime drinking was confined to two hours between 12 noon and 2pm and in the evening there was no opening until 7pm - again with a 10.30pm close. Meanwhile most shops were closed all day on Sunday - even at Christmas-time.

Above: *Santa Claus arrives in New George Street to start the Spooner's Christmas campaign.* Right: *St Andrew's and the Co-op in festive mode.*

Plymouth's Lord Mayors of the late-Fifties and Sixties

1955-56	Edwin Broad
1956-57	William James Oats
1957-58	Leslie Francis Paul
1958-59	George John Wingett
1959-60	Percy Washbourn
1960-61	Frederick John Scott
1961-62	Arthur Goldberg
1962-63	Henry George Mason
1963-64	Henry Pillar Pattinson
1964-65	Thomas Harold Watkins
1965-66	Percival Dorton Pascho
1966-67	Thomas HL Stanbury
1967-68	Frank Chapman
1968-69	Ivor Clarence Lowe
1969-70	George Ernest Hillyer Creber

Plymouth's MPs of the late-Fifties and Sixties

1955   Joan Vickers, Devonport (C)
        Hon. Jacob Astor, Sutton (C)
1959   Joan Vickers, Devonport (C)
        Ian Fraser, Sutton (C)
1964   Dame Joan Vickers, Devonport (C)
        Ian Fraser, Sutton (C)
1966   Dame Joan Vickers, Devonport (C)
        David Owen, Sutton (L)

Above: *Outside Redcot, our first Sixties home in Plymouth, May 1964.* Left: *My first local book, produced with help from the inspirational Audrey Hosier at Hyde Park Primary School in 1965.*

ACKNOWLEDGEMENTS

Many of the images that appear in this book have been supplied by readers of my Looking Back column in the Herald. In some instances they were photographs that had originally been taken for the paper back in the Fifties and Sixties, but in others they are simply happy snaps that have captured the essence of the era. These wonderfully evocative shots were, more often than not, unplanned and unposed, and yet they have a magical quality which adds much to this review.

The archives of the Herald and Western Morning News have also been immensely useful - thanks go to Alan Qualtrough, Bill Martin, Ian Wood and Pete Holgate. The bulk of this material is now curated by the Plymouth Barbican Trust's South West Image Bank at 25 Parade, on the Barbican - thanks there go to the Directors and their archivist Stacey Dyer.

The Plymouth Central Library Local Studies Department and the Plymouth City Museum and Art Gallery have also been very helpful. Dingles and the Plymouth Co-operative Society have been a valuable source of material. So too have old books, tourist guides, brochures, and souvenir programmes.

From a practical and personal perspective, I'd also like to express very grateful thanks to my publisher Clare (who is also my best friend and long-suffering wife), mother-in-law Patricia Greathead and long term friend and New Street colleague, Rob Warren, all of whom have read this looking for typos and other irritants. Thanks too to Doreen Mole, who keeps all my Looking Back bits and pieces in order.

Meanwhile, the A-Z list of those individuals who have sent me photographs over the last fifteen years or so - photographs that have helped make this book what it is - is once again a very long one, I only hope I haven't left anyone out!

And just before I mention anyone else I need to say a big thank you to Roy Westlake and Bernard Mills for permission to use their excellent photographic images.

Right: Broad Park Road, Peverell - a rare, colour, Plymouth street scene from the Sixties taken by an Australian relative in late 1964. Below: The author with his visiting grandparents, Stewart and Olive Robinson, and mother Brenda, pet whippet, Breeze, outside the family home - 15 Broad Park Road c.1967.

With thanks to: Gary and Lisa Andrews, Mike Antonucci, Francis Baker, Phil Barrow, Victor Barton, Ian Bickle, Joe Biddle, Guy Belshaw, Tony Benwell, Robin Blythe-Lord, Margaret Bond, John and Sylvia Boulden, Geoff Bowden, Tom Bowden, Chris Brant, Graham and Pat Brooks, Jean Brown, Paul Burtnyk, Dessie Carnell, Derek Carter, Robert Cattrall, Tim Charlesworth, Jean Chapman, Mina Chapman, Arthur Clamp, Peter Coleman, Fred Colton, Roger Compton, Bob Cook, Mike Cox, Harvey Crane, Bernice Dann, Maurice Dart, Sue Down, Brian Elliott, Andy Endacott, Marilyn Endacott, Dennis Escott, Guy Fleming, Dougie Flood, Arthur Folland, Michael Foot, Edna Furze, Brian Gadd, Daryle Gay, Crispin Gill, Duncan Godefroy, Keith Gorman, Tom Greaves, Michael Greenwood, Jim Griffin, Mike Griffiths, Terry Guswell, Nick Hales, Audrey Harrison, Gary Hayes, Hatti Hayne, Barry Henderson, Ron Hellyer, Ken Hill, Norman Hine, Derek Hiscock, Graham Hobbins, Tom Hobbs, Mike Hocking, Len and Joyce Hocking, Terry Horan, Robin Hoskins, John James, Daryl Jago, David Jennings, Ron Johns, Doreen Johnson, Steve Johnson, Sue Johns, Gillian Kent, David King, Alan Kittridge, Harley Lawer, Trevor Lear, Graham Little, Ray McSweeny, Ann Maddern, David May, Brian Moseley, Jimmy Moses, Frank Moulder, Jean Norsworthy, Sid Oliver, Pete Organ, Babs Owen, Cynthia Palmer, Mike Parriss, May Parson, Alan Pease, Joe Pengelly, Jean Perkins, Valerie Pilgrim, John Pinch, Frank Pocock, Merv Pollard, Bob Pratt, Jan Pritchard, Denise Putt, Des Robinson, Peter Rosevear, Colin Rowe, Janet Scoles, Charlie Sells, Dave Sharp, Hinton Sheryn, Peter Skinnard, Gordon Sparks, Jeanette Simpson, Reg Smith, Tina Southgate, Ray Steer, Len Stevens, Joan Stopperton, Derek Tait, Peter Taylor, Art Thomas, Mike Tibbs, Roy Todd, Sid Tonkin, David Tozer, Gerry Tucker, Don Tucker, Mike Turpitt, Chris Uren, Peter and Joy Vittle, Shirley Walker, John Walters, Jimmy Warren, Rob Warren, Peter Warrren, Gerald Wasley, Peter Waterhouse, Tony Way, Mike White, Peter Williamson, Mary Wills, Jonathan Wood, George and Dave Woolaway, Sonia Wright, and Mike Yeats.

Chris Robinson *October 2012*

BIBLIOGRAPHY

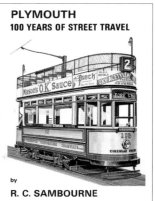
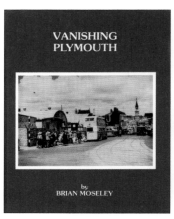

A Brief History of Plymouth Hospitals - **John Grier & Doreen Mole,** Old Plymouth Society (2004)

A Century and a Half of Savings - **Crispin Gill,** Plymouth, Devonport and Cornwall Trustee Savings Bank (1968)

A Century of Plymouth: Events, People and Places over the last 100 years – **Guy Fleming,** Sutton Publishing Ltd (2000)

All About Argyle 1903-1963 – **WS Tonkin,** Diamond Jubilee Book (1963)

Anderton and Rowland's Illusion & Reality – **Kevin Scrivens & Stephen Smith,** Fairground Heritage Trust (2008)

Archie Ballard, the Pier Piper of Plymouth - **George Male,** Ballard Trust (1994)

The Argyle Book - **Terry Guswell & Chris Robinson,** Pen & Ink (2002)

Argyle Classics - **Harley Lawer,** Green Books, Plymouth (1988)

Christmas Cheer annuals - **Crispin Gill,** Plymouth Guild of Community Service (1960-68)

The Complete Beatles Chronicle - **Mark Lewisohn,** Chancellor Press (1992)

Devon at the Cinema: An Illustrated History of Cinema Going – **Gordon Chapman,** Devon Books (2000)

Devonport Dockyard Railway – **Paul Burkhalter,** Twelveheads Press (1996)

Devonport Dockyard Story – **Lt Cdr Ken Burns,** Maritime Books (1984)

Elizabethan Plymouth – **Chris Robinson,** Pen & Ink (2002)

Fleet History of Plymouth Corporation and Plymouth Citybus Limited – The P.S.V

From Rattles to Radio, A History of Plymouth City Police Force, **Ernest Dickaty,** type-script (1977)

A History of Devonport – **Chris Robinson,** Pen & Ink (2010)

A History of Plymouth: And Her Neighbours – **C.W. Bracken,** Underhill (Plymouth) Ltd (1931)

Images of Plymouth – **Tom Bowden,** Sutton Publishing (2006)

Images of England: Plymouth – **Derek Tait,** Tempus Publishing Ltd (2003)

The Making of the University of Plymouth – **Alston Kennerley,** University of Plymouth

Naval Heritage in The West: Part I, II & III – **Andy Endacott** (1986, 1987, 1988)

Newton Abbot to Plymouth – **Vic Mitchell & Keith Smith,** Middleton Press (2001)

150 Years of the Co-operative in Plymouth – **Chris Robinson,** Pen & Ink (2009)

Oval Racing in Devon and Cornwall – **Andrew Weltch,** Tempus (2003)

 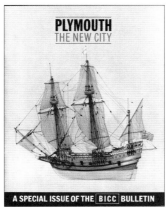 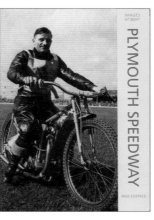 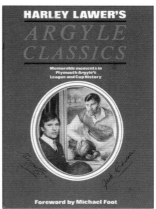 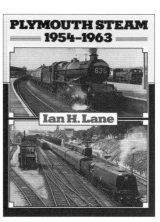

Playbill: A History of Theatre in the Westcountry – **Harvey Crane**, Macdonald and Evans Ltd (1980)

Plymouth Argyle: The Complete Record - **Ryan Danes**, Breedon Books (2009)

Plymouth: The New City - **DG Denoon ed.**, British Insulated Callender's Cables Limited (1964)

Plymouth: A New History – **Crispin Gill**, Devon Books (1993)

Plymouth: As Time Draws On Vols 1 & 2 – **Chris Robinson**, Pen & Ink Publishing (1985, 1988)

Plymouth College, The First Hundred Years – **Chris Robinson**, Pen & Ink Publishing (2005)

Plymouth Cricket Club 1857-2007 – **Phil Barrow**, Plymouth CC (2007)

Plymouth in Pictures – **Crispin Gill**, W J Holman Ltd (1968)

Plymouth in the Forties and Fifties - **Chris Robinson**, Pen & Ink Publishing (2011)

Plymouth: Maritime City in Transition – **Brian Chalkley, David Dunkerley, Peter Gripaios**, David & Charles (1991)

Plymouth: Official Guide – The Entertainments and Publicity Department of the City Council, Underhill Ltd (1957-69)

Plymouth: Ocean Liner, Port of Call – **Alan Kittridge**, Twelveheads Press (1993)

Plymouth Profile - **Uncredited**, Pyramid Press, London (c1966)

Plymouth: Pictures from the Past – **Guy Fleming**, The Devonshire Press Ltd (1995)

Plymouth River: A History of the Laira and Cattewater – **Crispin Gill**, Devon Books (1997)

Plymouth Speedway – **Paul Eustace**, Tempus Publishing Ltd (2006)

Plymouth to St. Austell – **Vic Mitchell & Keith Smith**, Middleton Press (2001)

Plymouth Vision of a Modern City – **Jeremy Gould,** English Heritage (2010)

Plymouth Yesterday Today – **Vic Saundercock** (1989)

Plymouth 100 Years of Street Travel – **R.C. Sambourne**, Glasney Press (circa 1970)

Plymouth 1848 - 1958 – **Crispin Gill**, Plymouth Y.M.C.A. (1958)

Plymouth's Historic Barbican – **Chris Robinson**, Pen & Ink Publishing (2007)

Royal Visits to Devon and Cornwall: Images from the WMN and Evening Herald 1900 - 2000 – **John Van Der Kiste**, Halsgrove (2002)

Scouting in Plymouth 1908 - 1982 – **Graham E. Brooks and Arthur L. Clamp**, P.D.S. Printers Ltd (1982)

The Second Book of Plymouth - **W. Best Harris**, Oakfield Press (circa 1960)

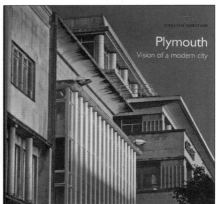

Ships in Plymouth Sound – **Sydney Goodman**, Halsgrove (1999)

Showmen of the Past: Hancocks of the West – **Kevin Scrivens & Stephen Smith**, New Era Publications (2006)

Speedway in the South-West – **Tony Lethbridge**, Tempus Publishing Inc (2003)

Steam Around Plymouth – **Bernard Mills**, Tempus Publishing Ltd (2003)

The Story of Plymouth – **R.A.J Walling**, London Westaway Books (1950)

Sutton Harbour – **Crispin Gill**, Devon Books (1997)

The Tamar Road Suspension Bridge - **Uncredited**, Cleveland Bridge & Engineering Co. (1962)

300 Years Devotion to Duty – **Andy Endacott** (1991)

Union Street – **Chris Robinson,** Pen & Ink (2000)

Victorian Plymouth: As Time Draws On – **Chris Robinson**, Pen & Ink Publishing (1991)

T. Whitelegg and Sons': Cavalcade of Shows – **Guy Belshaw**, New Era publications (2005)